"Providing an ultra-luxury experience involves making your service personal. The more personal, the more impactful. *Relationomics* is a guidebook to assist leaders in shaping stronger teams and cultivating connectivity, both internally and externally, and crafting a healthy work environment."

Horst Schulze, chairman emeritus, Capella Hotel Group;
chairman/CEO, WP Hospitality Group;
former president, Ritz-Carlton

"Everything good in life comes to us through relationships. Growth, maturity, and productivity are all outcomes of healthy relationships. If you want your organization to thrive relationally, I highly recommend you get a copy of *Relationomics*."

Andy Stanley, author, communicator, and founder,
North Point Ministries

"Good relationships make the world go around. That's true in life, and in business. Dr. Ross understands the value of cultivating deep and meaningful relationships in our business endeavors and provides us with an excellent guidebook for doing just that in *Relationomics*. Practical and thoughtful, *Relationomics* is a fantastic resource for leaders."

Dan T. Cathy, CEO, Chick-fil-A

"Healthy relationships drive business. To be effective and productive, people must work together as a team and love one another like family. In *Relationomics*, Dr. Ross has captured the principles and practices of relational maturity that will power your business. This book should be in every manager's toolbox."

Cheryl Bachelder, former CEO, Popeyes Louisiana
Kitchen, Inc.; author, *Dare to Serve*

"In the age of ever-expanding mega corporations, the tendency has been to focus on efficiency and emotionless transactions. In our effort to get the best price or the most productivity, we have destroyed the fabric of what brings people together to serve something larger than ourselves, and accomplish more than we ever thought possible. *Relationomics* brings this home in a very powerful way. Dr. Ross communicates complex topics in a conversational manner that will impact leaders at every level in your organization."

Scott MacLellan, CEO, TouchPoint Support Services,
Morrison Community Living,
and Bateman Community Living

"To be effective, leaders must create environments conducive for collaboration among people of diverse backgrounds, perspectives, and beliefs. If you want to gain clarity and unity in your organization, then *Relationomics* will help you get there."

Richard Cox, vice president of business operations,
Cox Automotive

"This book should come with a warning label for leaders. Because if you read and apply the principles contained within *Relationomics*, it could quite possibly change your view of relationships and business."

Duane Cummings, founder, the Speakers Guild
of America; former CEO, Leadercast

"In a franchise setting, nothing is more important than healthy relationships. Everything flourishes or falters based on the nature of relationships. If you want to enhance your relationships and drive business, then *Relationomics* provides both the insights and the practical principles to make that happen."

James Collins, US vice president and general manager, McDonald's

"Whether you are in an academic institution or a corporate setting, it is critical to provide safe and healthy environments in which people can learn, grow, and be productive. *Relationomics* will equip leaders to provide such environments and elevate the performance of their teams."

Linda Livingstone, PhD, president, Baylor University

"Relationship catalyzes growth. This message is transformative. If you want to build healthy teams, retain customers, and grow your business, *Relationomics* is a must-read book!"

Scott Beck, CEO, Gloo

"*Relationomics* hits the target and fans the flame for reimagining leadership. Providing rich insights, it connects the dots between the importance of surrounding ourselves with remarkable people and the necessity of intentionally and boldly growing those relationships."

Ron Dunn, president and CEO, CarpetsPlus COLORTILE; founder/director, One Thing for Men

"Whether leading a company, a team member, or an entrepreneur, this book offers a guaranteed recipe for sustained growth and prosperity. I've never felt so in touch with an author and his authenticity and humility as I have reading *Relationomics*."

Bob Littell, Chief NetWeaver

"Healthy relationships create healthy business. If you want to know how to inspire your teams, coach for maximum performance, and create a compelling culture, then *Relationomics* is a must-read."

Tim Leveridge, vice president and investor relations officer, The Coca-Cola Company

RELATIONOMICS

RELATIONOMICS

BUSINESS POWERED BY RELATIONSHIPS

DR. RANDY ROSS

BakerBooks

a division of Baker Publishing Group
Grand Rapids, Michigan

© 2019 by Remarkable Movement, LLC

Published by Baker Books
a division of Baker Publishing Group
PO Box 6287, Grand Rapids, MI 49516-6287
www.bakerbooks.com

Special edition ISBN 978-0-8010-9481-1

Printed in the United States of America

Library of Congress Cataloging-in-Publication Data
Names: Ross, Randy (Randall C.), 1959– author.
Title: Relationomics : business powered by relationships / Dr. Randy Ross.
Description: Grand Rapids, MI : Baker Books, [2019] | Includes bibliographical references.
Identifiers: LCCN 2018026527 | ISBN 9780801093937 (cloth)
Subjects: LCSH: Management. | Organizational effectiveness. | Organizational behavior.
Classification: LCC HD31 .R7245 2019 | DDC 658—dc23
LC record available at https://lccn.loc.gov/2018026527

The author is represented by The Christopher Ferebee Agency, www.christopherferebee.com.

19   20   21   22   23   24   25   7   6   5   4   3   2   1

To the love of my life, LuAnne, who continuously inspires me to create value for others, sharpens me relationally, encourages me to be my best, challenges me to apply what I teach, shows me unconditional love, brightens my world, and makes a beautiful "billboard."

CONTENTS

FOREWORD

Over many years, I've worked with and observed great leaders across a wide variety of organizations and industries. Many of them have discovered that when the people they serve are engaged at work and treated well, they will treat their customers well in turn. This results in happy customers who come back, content shareholders, and a thriving business.

The best leaders know that healthy relationships are the secret to great results and human satisfaction. Leaders who invest time and resources in serving, caring for, and developing their people see a noticeable difference in employee morale and engagement as well as in improved financial performance. The interesting thing to me is how many leaders say they would like this kind of culture but can't seem to spend the time and energy needed to get the *people* part right.

Leadership is about creating a nurturing environment in which your people can connect and collaborate. Life is not a solo sport. Every person must work effectively with both internal and external customers in order to be successful at what they do. The best leaders serve their people by modeling positive behavior. These serving leaders create both great relationships *and* results.

Randy Ross agrees. In *Relationomics*, he makes a compelling case for healthy relationships by calling out negative elements that can stifle people's growth and offering principles you can apply both at work and at home that will transform the way people relate to one another.

Relationomics contains practical wisdom and proven methods for untangling the biggest challenges facing today's business leaders. If you want to craft a compelling culture in which team members are inspired to bring their best to work every day, read this book!

Ken Blanchard
Chief Spiritual Officer of the Ken Blanchard Companies
Coauthor of *The New One Minute Manager*
and *Servant Leadership in Action*

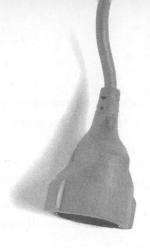

FOCUS ON THE FUNDAMENTALS:
INTENTIONALITY

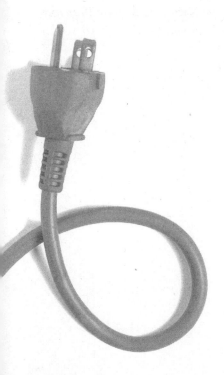

ONE

THIS IS A RELATIONSHIP!

The quality of a person's life is in direct proportion to their commitment to excellence, regardless of their chosen field of endeavor.

—Vince Lombardi

Most leaders believe the purpose of business is to make money. The best leaders are those who know that the real purpose of business is to make a difference in the lives of those they encounter. If the sole reason for a business to exist is simply to make money, people will figure that out and will soon cease to support that endeavor. But when a business truly seeks to create value for those it serves, it will most certainly make money. Because people will gladly pay full price for those things that they deem bring true value to life. And when an organization strives to make the lives of those they encounter just a little better, it will create a positive wake in the world. Those who are impacted by that wake will not only become faithful followers but also spread the word to increase the tribe.

Likewise, when organizations put people above profits, their priorities produce rich dividends both relationally and economically. For the heart of any business is its people. Thriving organizations are powered by people. And profitable organizations serve people well, both internally and externally. The healthier the relationships between these people, the better the business.

Unfortunately, few organizations promote healthy relationships. Some assume most people know how to build healthy relationships. For others, healthy relationships fall far behind other priorities on the scorecard. Culture is simply not a primary focus. Many organizations invest far more in their products and processes than in their people. As a result, relationships languish, customer service is mediocre, and conflict abounds. Poor relationships will almost always lead to poor performance.

This book is a modest effort to move relationships in the marketplace in a slightly more positive direction. It's my hope that the principles set forth within these pages will give leaders helpful fodder to guide them toward healthier relationships. The best businesses I have experienced are powered by healthy relationships. At the same time, I believe that the context of business is a fertile field in which healthy relationships can be cultivated and grown. Healthy relationships lead to healthier and happier lives. When people are healthy and happy, business flourishes.

Relationship catalyzes growth. No place is this more evident than in business. People want to grow. Companies want to grow. But growth is a by-product of healthy relationships. And the stark reality is that most business environments simply are not conducive to the cultivation of healthy relationships. Because of this, people suffer and, therefore, businesses suffer. Engagement falters and productivity is limited to less-than-optimal levels because few have prioritized and mastered the principles necessary to create vibrant, thriving relationships. Organizations don't get the results they desire because their leaders don't lead well relationally.

> **Relationship catalyzes growth.**

Practicing healthy relational principles to drive business may seem to be common sense, but I can assure you that it's not common practice. The practices necessary to move relationships from superficial to substantive are rarely commonly applied in business settings. Thus, there is a pressing need to focus on the fundamentals.

In July 1961, the Green Bay Packers were gathered for the first day of training camp. The previous season had ended badly as the Packers had squandered a lead late in the fourth quarter, losing the NFL championship to the Philadelphia Eagles. The brutal loss had haunted the team for the entire off-season. Now training camp offered hope for a fresh start. But before camp could get started, the players had to face their fiery coach as he set the framework and laid out the expectations for their workouts. Thirty-eight athletes, many of them half their coach's age and twice his size, were openly anxious and slightly unnerved as Vince Lombardi entered the room.

Lombardi stood in front of them. With football in hand, he looked around the room at the silent assemblage for what seemed like an eternity. Then, extending the pigskin in front of him in his right hand, he spoke five words that clarified his coaching philosophy. He simply said, "Gentlemen, this is a football."

With those words, he began a tradition of annually starting from scratch and taking nothing for granted. It wasn't meant to be insulting. It was necessary. It was basic. It was clarifying. It was . . . inspirational.

> **Practicing healthy relational principles to drive business may seem to be common sense, but I can assure you that it's not common practice.**

The players, eager to advance their games, wanted to hear how their coach planned to get the team back to being a championship contender. They were reeling from the realization that they had come within minutes of winning on the biggest stage their sport could offer. They were preoccupied with the prize. Lombardi knew that what they really needed was a refresher course. If they didn't get back to the basics of blocking and tackling, then their greatest desire would be nothing more than a pipe dream. So, Lombardi's methodical coverage of the fundamentals continued for the duration of training camp.

At one point, during yet another rudimentary instructional session, Max McGee, the Packer's Pro Bowl wide receiver, joked, "Uh, Coach, could you slow down a little? You're going too fast for us." The attempt at levity brought a smile to Lombardi's face, but his obsession with the fundamentals remained undeterred. He was steadfast in his commitment to practice to perfection the most foundational elements of the game. Consequently, his team became the best in the league at mastering the basics that everyone else took for granted.

Six months later, the Green Bay Packers annihilated the New York Giants, winning 37–0 and clinching the NFL championship. Vince Lombardi would never lose in the playoffs again. He won five NFL championships in a span of seven years. He never coached a team with a losing record and is still considered one of the greatest coaches to ever lead a team onto the football field.[1]

This obsession over the basics has been a hallmark of many successful coaches. John Wooden, the great legend of the hard court, was known to start every season by teaching his players how to put on their socks and tie their shoes. That's as elementary as you can get. Likewise, Nick Saban, the famed coach of the Alabama Crimson Tide, never worries about the scoreboard but instead focuses keenly on the process. If anyone were to have a reason to start with the end in mind, it would be Nick. Walking in the wake of Paul "Bear" Bryant, he is poised to capture more national titles than any other college coach in history. Yet he refuses to speculate about the future. He is doggedly focused on being in the present and doing what is necessary to make each and every moment count. He knows that if you do what is necessary to prepare properly today, tomorrow will take care of itself. If you master the basics and bring your absolute best to every minute of practice, then you will be ready for the game on Saturday. And when you bring your absolute best, your best will be enough.

It's always about the basics, no matter how far we may advance. Good coaches focus on the fundamentals. Good business leaders do the same. And nothing is more basic than how we relate to one another. If we get this relational piece right, then growth will naturally follow. Healthy relationships will lead to the growth of individuals, the growth of teams, and the growth of enterprises.

You may be feeling a bit like Max McGee, ready to respond with a big, "No duh! Can we please move on?" The thought of such a response brings a smile to my face. Hey, I get it. We all think we have mastered the basics of communication and interpersonal relationships. If not, then how did we get to where we are today? After all, you might say, you can't be a leader without some semblance of social grace and relational acuity.

> **It's always about the basics, no matter how far we may advance.**

Fair enough. But I remain undeterred in my pursuit of this point. What got you to where you are may not take you to the next level. Individual achievement and regular promotions do not necessarily equip you to connect deeply relationally and to effectively lead others.

I led a team of recruiters for a large regional group in the mortgage field earlier in my career. My team and I were tasked with the responsibility of determining who might be successful as mortgage originators. It was a role I enjoyed, and I had the privilege of meeting many wonderful people in the process. But I wish I had a dollar for every time I heard a candidate say, "I'm perfectly suited for this job because I'm a people person." Occasionally, I was unsuccessful in demonstrating self-restraint and blurted out what I was thinking. "You're a people person, huh? That's interesting. What exactly does being a people person mean?"

I can honestly say I never received a response that increased my level of comfort with any of those candidates;

they weren't actually the people persons they thought they were. They each had this mistaken notion of what being a people person actually meant. Interestingly, each one included the word *love* in their explanations but was unable to clearly and articulately describe what that looked like in real life. So, what's the point?

You may indeed be a leader. But the sad reality is that many leaders do not lead well. We assume that somewhere along the line, everyone learned how to play well in the sandbox with others. We also assume life experiences have refined relational capacities. Those assumptions would often be wrong about others and they would also likely be wrong about us. People suffer and organizations flounder with less-than-stellar cultures and meager results when we neglect to address the essentials that lead to healthy relationships.

Think about the following questions. Then write either "yes" or "no," along with any additional thoughts, in the space provided.

❯❯ GAINING TRACTION: Questions for Consideration & Application

1. Do projects in your organization occasionally get side-tracked, or even derailed, due to interpersonal conflict?

2. Is unresolved conflict leading to lack of unity among team members?

3. Does a low level of trust cause unnecessary friction among team members?

4. Do you lose too many good people to other organizations?

5. When there is a vacuum in communication, do people tend to assume the worst rather than believe the best?

6. Do you struggle with territorialism and silos within the organization?

7. Do work groups compete with one another when it comes to allocation of resources?

8. Would you like to increase collaboration among teams?

9. Would you like to reduce turnover?

10. Would you like to attract better talent?

11. Would you like for your people to experience greater meaning and fulfillment in their work?

12. Would you like to elevate the morale and productivity of your teams?

13. Would you like to create movements of good within your organization that inspire team members to bring their best to work each day?

14. Would you like your folks to be deeply committed to your organization's vision, mission, and purpose?

15. Would you like for everyone to be kind and play nice together?

16. Would you like to elevate performance?

17. Is there a need for honest developmental feedback?

18. Would you like for everyone to look forward to coming to work each day, knowing they are part of a team committed to their personal growth and the growth of the organization?

If you answered yes to any of these questions, then maybe it's time we get back to the basics.

What I propose to do in the following pages is extend to you some fundamental and profound ideas and simply say, "Ladies and gentlemen, this is a relationship."

TWO

THE GREAT DECEPTION

The greatest way to live with honor in this world is to be what we pretend to be.

—Socrates

Most people have a desire to grow, but very few know how to do it. Growth requires change, and most people are change resistant. Growth occurs best when people are part of a community. This is because relationships force us to change things about ourselves that simply don't work in real life. Relationships also provide us with the opportunity to move toward healing, wholeness, and maturity.

We each have a certain way we like to view ourselves and like others to see us. But that way doesn't always jibe with how others experience us. This incongruity could be described as a blind spot, or it could be a more menacing manifestation of self-delusion. Either way, we don't have the capacity to see things about ourselves the way others close to us do. And sometimes the things they see in us, that we don't see in ourselves, are detrimental to relationships.

This tendency, if we are not in strong relationships, causes us to create either grandiose perceptions or demoralizing devaluations of ourselves. These skewed perceptions create a chasm between others and us that prevents connectivity and promotes chaos. Only relationship can bridge the chasm. Healthy relationships can deflate any fanciful fantasies we have about ourselves and provide objective insights to help move us toward maturity. Healthy relationships can also provide the encouragement we need to overcome our insecurities and bolster the self-confidence required to address our greatest fears.

Maturity is driven by self-awareness and requires accurate self-perception, authenticity, and the humility to make the necessary changes to engage effectively in community. In short, maturity is measured by how well we relate to others. The unfortunate reality is that most people don't build deep relationships in which they seek honest feedback from others, nor do they move constructively into difficult relationships with the intention to change themselves for the better. More often than not, conflict-laden relationships are exacerbated by image control on the part of one or both parties. When this posturing takes place, it's usually accompanied by elaborate attempts to bring about change in the other person, with very little personal introspection. These attempts can range from simple deflection to outright demands and manipulation. Each is intended to avoid the painful process of taking personal responsibility for making the changes necessary to move toward deeper, more mature relationships.

Posturing, self-protection, and self-promotion are all toxic for relationships. They preclude authenticity, which is the ability to embrace ourselves as we are in our entirety. It's the capacity to understand and leverage our strengths, being honest about our shortcomings, and the willingness to be transparent about both with others. Authenticity and transparency have tremendous power in promoting healthy relationships. But before we take a deeper look at that, let's first address some of the hurdles we have to clear in order to pursue more meaningful relationships.

> **Maturity is measured by how well we relate to others.**

The Self-Help Conundrum

A significant barrier to healthy relationships is the one built by those who market personal improvement materials. It's the great Self-Help Conundrum. Go into any bookstore and you will find shelves upon shelves of books that fall into this genre. Their promise is that if you read this, it will make you a better that. Practice these principles and you will become more powerful. Do such and such and you will get what you really want. Take these seven steps to become your best self.

But each guide to greatness will, in all likelihood, leave out one essential element: the power of others in the process. We have long been told, "You can do it on your own." "Pull yourself up by your bootstraps." "Make something of yourself!" "You, alone, should be the master of your destiny."

The intent is good. The messages are meant to empower. The process is prescriptive. But more often than not, such guides miss the interpersonal dynamic and, therefore, have limited value in driving change to help us better ourselves.

Don't get me wrong. I'm all about taking personal responsibility. The world is filled with far too many victims who think that somehow the world owes them something. Rather than sitting passively and waiting for someone else to bring about a desired change, we each must demonstrate personal initiative and intentionality in the pursuit of maturity. I believe we should all seek to be and bring about the change we wish to see in the world. A steadfast commitment to personal growth requires intense effort. But the reality is that *we cannot do it all by ourselves*. That's not how we are wired and that's not how the world works. We are all interconnected. By nature, we are relational creatures and relationships help hone us to maturity.

For growth to take place, we have to do more than simply expose people to good information. If exposure to good information alone were the key to growth, then the internet should have solved the world's relational problems by now. With a few strokes on the keyboard, we can have a world of information at our fingertips that should resolve any relational crisis. Yet relational crises still abound. Obviously, access to information alone does not provide everything necessary to resolve real-life relational issues.

> **For growth to take place, we have to do more than simply expose people to good information.**

We have all heard powerful, inspirational speeches and been moved in the moment. Yet how often have you, after

30

having heard such a moving message, forgotten the main points of that very address before you even reach your car in the parking lot? I know I certainly have. So access to good information does not necessarily lead to change, no matter how inspirational the information may be. That is why so many of us have attended great conferences, with powerful speakers, and taken lots of notes only to discover months later that nothing has changed. Let me be overtly redundant and say it again: access to good information alone does not guarantee personal growth.

To illustrate, let me use a common corporate dilemma. A source of great frustration for many organizations is based on the mistaken notion that people who desire to grow will self-activate. Companies spend millions of dollars conceiving and creating learning management systems. They operate under the Field of Dreams Myth that posits, "If we build it, they will come." They curate content and amass resource libraries, all designed to help people grow in their knowledge and competencies. Then, much to the chagrin of those in training and development, when these elaborate training vessels are launched, very few people show up and even fewer still experience real growth by coming aboard. Most neither actively retrieve nor warmly receive content that could be utilized to foster personal and professional growth. What becomes painfully clear is that outside of using the learning management system to drive compliance-related training, these reservoirs are rarely visited. Like ghost towns abandoned by prospectors before they reach the mother lode buried within, these elaborate libraries, with their voluminous content, rest peacefully undisturbed by the masses.

Pushing content through a *pipeline* is rarely effective. A pipeline is designed to deliver a specific product to a single end user. Pipelines fail to create a conversation in which relationships are strengthened and growth in community results.

Platforms, however, create relationships. The true value of a learning system doesn't reside in the repository of information but rather in the relationships fostered between those who interact around the content. The platform provides the stage on which growth takes place, with the content playing a supportive role. The beauty of a learning system is in the community that it fosters and nourishes. The relationship, not the content, is key.

As you can see, there is a vast difference between the way a pipeline and a platform each approach content delivery. Traditional learning systems are essentially pipelines. There is a reservoir of content, which is pushed from a repository to a recipient. It's a one-way flow of information that the sender hopes the recipient will ingest, thus providing the diet of information for growth to take place. But, devoid of relationship, it rarely garners the intended result.

A platform, conversely, provides a stage for interaction for those who have been enlisted in a learning community. Information flows freely back and forth, allowing all participants to move fluidly between the modalities of learning, applying, and teaching. This learning triangle produces an environment of friendship and reinforcement. Because information is shared in the context of community and encouragement, learning takes place at a rapid pace and application is celebrated among members of the learning community. Platform business models tap into the innate human desire to help others, creating value and inspiring additional investment in the growth of another.

Therefore, the goal of any learning system should be to facilitate healthy relationships around content instead of merely seeking to deliver content itself. Systems designed around platform principles support the cultivation of relationships on multiple levels as the community participates in the growth process. While platforms efficiently deliver quality content, the main focus is to capitalize on the compounding effect that is generated when a number of people are interacting and offering insights and best practices around specific content.

> **The goal of any learning system should be to facilitate healthy relationships around content instead of merely seeking to deliver content itself.**

In doing so, platforms produce a flywheel effect, generating the impetus for personal development based on the power of relational connectivity. Growth is best facilitated within the context of learning communities. Self-help leaves us alone in a vacuum of disconnectedness. It's a fundamentally flawed assumption that people grow best in isolation, working things out on their own. Relationship catalyzes growth.

The Luciferian Lie

When we aren't moving into healthy relationships, we can fall prey to self-deception and the mistaken notion that we can make life work on our own. This is the great Luciferian Lie. Allow me to wax philosophical for a moment. Ancient religious literature tells the story of the creation of humankind. Whether or not you embrace this narrative of the creation account, it contains a powerful principle regarding the necessity of relationship to move toward maturity. According to these religious texts, God created the heavens and the earth and everything contained within them. Then he created man. But it was not good for man to be alone, so God made them male and female, as the pinnacle of his creative process. And he placed man and woman together in the Garden of Eden to enjoy each other's company, appreciate their relationship with him, and relish in the vast resources at their fingertips. God's intent was for them to flourish and experience a satisfying and fulfilling existence in community. Man and woman lived in a relationship with each other and with God that was pure and unadulterated. Their intimate community suffered no pretense. They were fully exposed and fully known to each other and lived in harmony with creation. It was, in a word, *paradise*.

But then something went horribly wrong. Lucifer appeared in the form of a serpent and enticed the woman. He questioned God's design for humans and his desire for humankind's fulfillment. The sly serpent suggested that God was withholding something good to which they were entitled. The fact was that God had provided them with everything they needed to experience the fullness of creation. But the one thing he had instructed them not to do was to eat from the tree of the knowledge of good and evil. His intent was not to deprive them but to protect them. They already and only knew everything that was good. Their lives were idyllic. What benefit could there possibly be in knowing evil? But the serpent was persuasive. Eating from this tree, he assured the woman, would make her like God himself. She wouldn't have to be in relationship with God. She could be "god." And it would be her expanded knowledge that would allow her to morph into the divine.

It was a lie. Eve was deceived. Adam remained silent. Though he had been the one who had firsthand knowledge of God's instructions, he, too, fell prey to the appealing proposition. Instead of stepping into the light and addressing the lie, he remained in the shadows and succumbed to the temptation of self-aggrandizement. Rather than remaining in a trusting relationship with the One who had given them life, they chose instead to take the path of self-promotion. They attempted to elevate both their knowledge and position by circumventing relationship. In doing so, they killed community and forfeited paradise. When the relationship was ruptured, Eden was lost.[1]

Contained within this narrative is a principle that speaks to the very core of human nature. Within each one of us is an innate desire to move toward enlightenment. The lie, however, is that enlightenment can be attained outside of community with others. This belief in the human capacity to move toward self-fulfillment outside of relationship is the hallmark of Luciferianism. Many are misled to believe that independence is the hallmark of maturity. It's not. Maturity means we live well with others in healthy, interdependent relationships.

Think about it. We were each born into a family. Our family was the community in which we learned how to relate to others. Each interaction with our parents and siblings shaped us. To a great extent, our values, beliefs, and behaviors were forged by our early interactions with our family. As we grew older, our circle of friends and acquaintances also grew. And every encounter helped crystalize what we believed to be true about ourselves, the world in general, and others. We grew because of relationships. And if we want to continue to grow, it will be because of relationships.

Understanding the Power of Relationships

Business is also about relationships. Relationships, through which those who have a need are linked with those who can supply, is an exchange of value that benefits both parties. In fact, relationships are the very foundation of business. And healthy relationships are always at the center of thriving businesses. I would go so far as to say that good business is never about simply making money. It's really about building relationships and making a difference in people's lives. The better you build relationships and the more value you create for others in those relationships, the more money you will make. The more personally you connect with others, the more your business will flourish.

I call it *relationomics*. Now, don't go look it up, because I made up that term! But *relationomics*, as I define it, is the study of the observable impact that relationships have on economic activity. It's an assessment of the value created by relationships as opposed to simply a fiscal transactional analysis. In the marketplace, a significant causal correlation exists between the strength of the relationship and the flow of resources. The stronger and healthier the relationship, the more productive and profitable the transactions between those parties tend to be.

On a personal level, if you want to be your best self, you need someone else speaking into your world through relationship.

For an athlete to fulfill her potential, she needs a relationship with a coach. For a student to maximize learning, he must have a relationship with a teacher or tutor. If you want to grow in your professional life, you'd best engage with a mentor. For us to move toward maturity, we need deep, healthy relationships with family and friends. We all need others to speak truth into our world. We may very well be the best person in the room, but we won't be our best self if we don't have others who are encouraging, challenging, and sharpening us.

Relationships significantly impact who we become. James P. Comer, professor of child psychiatry at the Yale Child Study Center, says, "No significant learning can occur without a significant relationship."[2] Working with schools in low economic areas, he found students struggling with frequent absences, lack of learning, and behavior issues. Rather than label the students as failures, he started with the viewpoint that their experiences resulted in a lack of performance, so he began to evaluate the students' school and home environments to determine what impact they had on learning. He found that students were coming to school without the proper skills to be successful.

> **We won't be our best self if we don't have others who are encouraging, challenging, and sharpening us.**

The strong relational bonds that help students develop the proficiencies to learn were not present. The social connectivity that had once been present in the communities and educational system had deteriorated. So, in 1968, he worked with parents, teachers, and administrators to create the School Development Program (SDP) to help schools recreate those social bonds and foster student development. And it worked.

The SDP caused a sharp increase in student achievement, accompanied by a decrease in behavioral issues. This SDP model has now been utilized in over a thousand schools throughout half of the United States. Each time stakeholders work together to foster child and adolescent development, it results in an improved school culture in which comfort, confidence, competence, and motivation to learn increase.

With that kind of success, you would think that opponents would give up, schools would focus on relationships, and we would move on to create more relationally connected learning environments. But that hasn't happened. Almost forty years after his groundbreaking work with the New Haven schools, improved educational practices have continued to focus on curriculum, instruction, assessment, and modes of service delivery. Insufficient attention has been paid to the impact relational bonds have on child and adolescent development. Instead, school systems continue to place the spotlight on the wrong issues to our own peril.[3]

Personal growth isn't simply about acquiring knowledge. It's about how we apply knowledge to enhance relationships. The Great Deception is the notion that we can ascend to greatness apart from relationship. The deception also encompasses the faulty premise that you can be a strong leader without healthy relationships. Don't fall for the lies. If you think leadership is a lonely proposition, then you're simply doing it wrong. Healthy relationships are the essence of leadership—and life.

Again, you may be thinking to yourself this is all elementary. And so it may seem. But how often have you fallen for any of the following fallacies?

- It's lonely at the top.
- You cannot be close to your people and lead them well.
- I have to keep my personal life and my professional life separate.
- It's hard to have close friendships at work.
- I can't let others see my weaknesses.
- Leadership is a lonely proposition.
- Asking for help is a sign of weakness.
- I can do this on my own. I don't need help.
- My people don't have to like me to follow me.
- I cannot let my people challenge me or they won't respect me.

Have you ever found yourself thinking or saying any of the sentiments above? If so, you have fallen for the lie. Buying into these beliefs will lead you down a path to loneliness and isolation, which inevitably leads to desperation. We definitely don't need any more desperate leaders among us in the marketplace.

The cure is community. The cure is relationship.

≫ GAINING TRACTION: Questions for Consideration & Application

1. How would you define maturity?

2. Why is the concept of self-help limited?

3. Why is exposure to good information alone not enough to spur growth?

4. Luciferianism is a belief system that promotes enlightenment, independence, and human progression. How would you assess this philosophical system as a means to personal development?

5. Why are authentic, transparent relationships necessary to catalyze growth?

6. Why is it so easy for leaders to find themselves isolated and without deep relationships?

THREE

MYOPIA IS NO UTOPIA

Very often a change of self is needed more than a change of scene.

—A. C. Benson

B efore you build, you have to assess the foundation to make sure it's solid and the footers are securely set on bedrock. Only then can you build with the assurance that your project will stand the test of time and remain steadfast through stormy seasons and shifting soil. While the vast majority of this book is about building the new, it's necessary for us to understand the influences that have bred an environment in which it's difficult to pursue healthy relationships.

The single greatest factor impeding healthy relationships is myopia. Myopia can best be described simply as shortsightedness. In ophthalmology, myopia is a visual defect in which distant objects appear blurred because their images are focused in front of the retina rather than on it, thereby creating nearsightedness. Objects that are close are clear, but those that are more remote remain blurred. The remedy is to reshape the lens through which one looks so that images are focused clearly on the retina to gain proper perspective.

In culture, myopia is often referred to as an inability to see into the future. It may be described as a lack of foresight or discernment. It could also be narrow-mindedness or the inability to see the wake that one leaves in the world. In this case, it refers to making choices today for reasons of personal comfort and convenience that may have long-lasting negative consequences on generations to come. This cultural myopia exchanges long-term value for short-term gain, saddling the next generation with the negative baggage of our bad decisions. This myopia can manifest itself in a variety of ways, from lack of environmental conscientiousness to the poor politics of partisanship, which sacrifices collaboration on the altar of petrified ideology (beliefs that have long been proven lifeless but have, nevertheless, hardened into stone).

Relationally speaking, myopia can best be described as a me-first mentality. It's the tendency to make choices based on what is best for me, with blatant disregard for how those choices may impact those around me. It's the result of an independent spirit, fostered by a society that is becoming increasingly disconnected. "Looking out for number one" has become the obsession of an obtuse generation. This inability to see beyond

> ❯ **Relationally speaking, myopia can best be described as a me-first mentality.**

42

self has led to the weakening of relational bridges and the fracturing of the foundation of society itself. Unless we make a conscientious attempt to correct the lens through which we look, our vision of the future will remain blurred. This me-first mentality shows up in the marketplace in a number of unhealthy ways. Let's explore just a few of these destructive perspectives.

Self-Protection: The Fear of Being Found Out

An executive-level leader I had the privilege of working with was struggling greatly in his relationships with his direct reports. His career as a sales leader had been stellar. He was a highly respected team member who had contributed significantly to the success of the organization as an individual contributor. He had performed spectacularly in his sales role, providing service to existing accounts and adding new clients to each territory over which he had been given responsibility. Because of his knowledge of the product lines and sales processes, he was tapped to give oversight to the sales organization. For about nine months, things ran smoothly. He gave general direction to the team and coached them on sales techniques that had made him successful. But then the relational gears began to grind and the sales engine began to stall. The team was losing momentum fast. Infighting among team members and frustration between sales and operations had led to a growing discontentment throughout the ranks. Critical relational lines were leaking emotional fluid. They had lost power to the engine and he had no idea how to jump-start it again.

The executive was bright, energetic, and articulate. He was a master of schmooze. He could light up any room with his humor and carried himself with poise in every social situation. By all appearances he was winsome and confident. But good times conceal what tough times reveal. There was a crack in his leadership capacity that was less noticeable until the pressure began to pry the team apart. While competent in the sales arena, he lacked the emotional intelligence to effectively read his team and lead them to relational health. He also lacked the emotional fortitude to wade into conflict and address the unhealthy behavior that had hijacked the team's performance.

As I coached him, a deep-seated secret began to surface, which crippled his effectiveness. In a moment of candor, he confessed that he labored under the nagging fear of eventually being exposed as a fraud. There was a single question that relentlessly pounded away at his confidence like a woodpecker on soft wood. The question that continually haunted him was this: "How long will it be until they discover that I am not all that I pretend to be?"

This single question drove him to create an elaborate system of self-protection through deflection. Whenever conflict would arise, he would seek to avoid it. He would minimize and dismiss it, hoping it would go away. He would make excuses for one, both, or all parties involved, equally distributing the blame while never effectively addressing the issues. Or he would ask someone else on the team to do the dirty work, only to have the tensions mount higher. He often acted out of fear. By not addressing the issues head on, he was only postponing the inevitable, allowing the situation to worsen.

His fear of being found out had effectively incapacitated him from providing the strong leadership his team needed.

Hiding behind a veneer of performance, he had learned to self-promote and self-protect. He had discovered how to distance himself from the dirt, so as not to get soiled. But, while protecting his appearance, he forfeited healthy relationships. Healthy relationships require authenticity and vulnerability. They also require the strength to move into difficult situations with the ability to speak the truth and, when necessary, deliver consequences to sideline bad behavior. Leadership requires us to roll up our sleeves and dig into the messiness of our humanity. But his fear had rendered him helpless to do the more difficult tasks of leadership.

The tendency to mask and cover weaknesses produces a pretense that prevents us from connecting deeply with others. When one cannot face oneself honestly, one cannot lead others effectively. When there is a delta between reality and the image we convey to others, we create pretense to fill the void. Pretense always requires self-protection to survive. We distance ourselves from others in order to hide our vulnerabilities. When we do this, we may think we are shielding ourselves from exposure, but we are really creating a chasm that prevents us from connecting with others in a meaningful way.

Possessing weaknesses is part of being human. Attempting to camouflage weaknesses is an act of futility. But acknowledging weaknesses and working on them is endearing and will garner both praise and support in healthy community. At the same time, self-acceptance is crucial in order to move in healthy ways with others. And authenticity is necessary for building open and trusting relationships. We will explore this more fully later.

Self-Promotion: Competition vs. Collaboration

Games are based on it. Society reinforces it. Enterprises attempt to leverage it. Some thrive in the face of it. Others pursue it at all cost. Yet countless others are damaged by it. I am talking about competition—the innate human tendency to strive against others in pursuit of a prize or place of prominence. For games to be fun, you have to have a winner and a loser. But the consequences of games, at least at the level at which most of us play, are essentially nonexistent. Even if you play in and win the Super Bowl, there is a long-lasting positive impact for only an extremely small number of people.

We compete because we love the thrill of the challenge and it gives us a way to compare ourselves to others. We all want to be seen as winners. But if our tendency toward competition causes us to self-promote to the point of disrespecting others or minimizing their contributions, then we can destroy collaboration.

This tendency toward competition is based on what I call the *ER Factor*. Whenever we attempt to position ourselves as being strong-*ER*, smart-*ER*, fast-*ER*, pretti-*ER*, wealthi-*ER*, wis-*ER*, or essentially bett-*ER* than others, we have assumed the role of the competitor. The ER Factor derives its name from the two elements that fuel competition—*ego* and *rivalry*. These two components drive competition, but they also destroy relationships. Think about it. If you are in a relationship with someone who must constantly prove themselves to be strong-*ER*, smart-*ER*, and bett-*ER* than you, it won't be too long until that relationship is ov-*ER*! No one likes to be forced to walk in the shadow of another. The ER Factor is the antithesis of servant leadership. It causes us to

46

seek what is best for ourselves and sacrifices relationships on the altar of self-promotion.

Similarly, many well-meaning organizations have leveraged this human tendency toward competition to spur elevated performance. Think of the proverbial sales challenge. The team or individual with the highest production gets the prize. Whether it's a piece of cut glass, a bonus, or a trip to an exotic destination, the race is on to beat everyone else. In this scenario, the organization thinks it's spurring elevated production. The reality is that it almost always results in unintended collateral damage. An individual or team that performs well may essentially block others from discovering their "secret sauce" or best practices to ensure their own victory. Collaboration is sacrificed in the wake of competition. While one individual or team may rise to the top, others may be floundering for lack of knowledge or resources that may be at the disposal of their competitors.

I watched this vividly illustrated in a large sales organization. The perennial winner of virtually every competition was a sales associate who had been in the industry for considerably longer than everyone else in the office. Due to her tenure and success, she had built a team of two assistants who did the majority of her calling and paperwork. Because of her success, those in operations tended to give her more latitude and even preferential treatment. Of course she was going to be more productive than the others who had to do all the work themselves and jockey for the attention of those in operations. But no one seemed to be bothered by the inequity. Corporate had set up the competition and everyone on the local level had all but acquiesced. Short of acknowledging her the winner at the start, everyone had assumed an inferior position. The competition was by all accounts counterproductive.

Imagine how much more impactful it could have been to have structured the work environment in such a way as to reward those who shared the most best practices. What if the enterprise had recognized those who spent time mentoring and coaching others to success? What if sharing the secret sauce was rewarded? Rather than silo and sequester resources, what if team members engaged in a collaborative interchange that elevated everyone's performance? Imagine how much more the organization would have benefited from such an approach.

I'm not suggesting all competition is bad. And I'm certainly not suggesting we bolster everyone's self-esteem by doling out trophies for just showing up. What I am saying is that you almost always garner more through collaboration than you ever will through competition, especially in high-stakes arenas. Competition, in its most effective form, should always be pursued not to best others but to bring the greatest value possible to your target audience. We compete not *against* others but *for* the growth and benefit of our clients, both internally and externally. If anything, we compete with ourselves in an attempt to bring more value to the table tomorrow than we did today, always seeking to improve on our best. And we collaborate with others to champion growth. An attitude of growth says, "I'm going to be better today than I was yesterday, and I'm only half as good today as I will be tomorrow!"

People As Pawns

Attitudes about the human component of business are changing. Identifiers such as *human capital* are being replaced by the terms *associate* and *team member*. And titles such as *Human Resources* are being changed to the *Office of People and Culture*. Along with the shift in nomenclature is a movement away from viewing people simply as assets of the organization.

> **You almost always garner more through collaboration than you ever will through competition.**

The tendency to see humans as assets was an unintended consequence of applying the *Principles of Scientific Management*. Introduced by Frederick Winslow Taylor shortly after the turn of the twentieth century, the Principles of Scientific Management were formulated to increase efficiency in factory work as America's economy moved from farm based to one primarily driven by manufacturing. On the farm, individuals learned certain skills necessary for daily survival. Apprenticeship was the means through which these skills were imparted, and they were often passed on through families for generations. Thus, individuals were most often known and identified by their vocation. Apprenticeship was personal and hands-on in nature. When work shifted from agrarian to manufacturing jobs in the city, individual identities based on heritage and specialization gave way to mass identification. Farmers, blacksmiths, clerks, merchants, and dairymen became factory workers. Work was standardized for operational excellence, and workers were seen as a part of the system or assets to be leveraged for maximum productivity.

Management replaced mentorship. Routine replaced relationship. While systemization brought greater productivity in many realms, it minimized the importance of the individual, reducing the workforce to cogs in a wheel.

The best management was seen as a true science, resting on clearly defined laws, rules, and principles as the foundation of efficiency. The individual was only as valuable as their willingness to relinquish their individual identity and step into the production line, where conformity led to productivity.

While serving as the predecessor to systems of process improvement and organizational efficiency like Lean Management and Six Sigma, the Principles of Scientific Management are essentially values-neutral. Values neutrality means that these principles carry little or no moral or ethical weight in and of themselves. In this system, value is seen as the elimination of waste, reducing production time and cost. The value to the customer is a defect-free item at a reduced cost. But such value does not necessarily carry with it a sense of corporate responsibility or individual morality. There is little redeeming value in a cheaper product if it in some way compromises the lives of those who produce it.

Let me explain. It's true that Frederick Taylor's management theories contributed significantly to increasing the productivity of early American factories. However, those very same principles of process efficiency were implemented to exterminate life in the Nazi concentration camps of World War II. The principles themselves have no moral or ethical sensibility. Applied within the context of a relationally healthy culture, the Principles of Scientific Management can be leveraged to reduce waste and improve quality. However, void of social responsibility and without an alignment of personal and organizational values, the very same principles can grind the workforce into automatons, manipulated by an organization without conscience.[1]

This is what many refer to as a "churn and burn" organizational culture. Everyone plays a role and, to the extent that they are willing to sacrifice self, each is promoted. Some refer to this as an "up or out" organizational approach. You either climb up the ladder, often at your own peril or at the expense of others, or you are forced out to find another ladder leaning against another wall. In this type of corporate culture, friendship among colleagues can be hard to find. Like salmon swimming upstream while avoiding a hungry bear, people in these work environments find it difficult to locate safe waters, where deeper relationships can be spawned. Jockeying and positioning for promotions often curtail collaboration. Self-protection and self-promotion abound. Deep relationships are scarce. People are moved around like pawns in a game of corporate chess and then sacrificed to protect the greater interest of the more valuable pieces on the board. All the while, some wonder why employee engagement statistics hover at such low levels.

Independence and Isolation

With the coming of the information age, the pendulum has now swung to an emphasis on individualism. The playing field has been leveled by the sheer fact that all the information one could possibly need is only a few keystrokes away. If it were information alone that we needed, we really wouldn't need one another anymore. Life-sustaining information was once passed from one generation to another. Such relational connectivity was imperative for survival. Now we only need access to the internet. We can gain access to information, conduct conference calls with team members globally, and provide webinars for clients without ever having to be face-to-face with anyone. Technology connects us to everyone and no one.

We can claim hundreds, if not thousands, of friends on Facebook and yet be truly known by no one. We can be connected in gigantic networks, such as LinkedIn, and still lack for productive business relationships. We can have a flock of followers on Twitter and never reveal anything personal or meaningful. It's the popularity parody. Technology has the ability to connect millions, while the million connections remain impersonal.

> **Technology connects us to everyone and no one.**

Technology has bred a spirit of both independence and isolation. Independence in that we really don't need others to show us or teach us anything. We can get access to everything we need to know all by ourselves. We don't seem to need a teacher, coach, mentor, or even parent to give us the information required to survive. Google allows us to explore every topic imaginable. YouTube entertains and shows us how to do things. Wikipedia provides collective intelligence.

At the same time, the nature of interpersonal communication has changed dramatically as well. Families sit together at the dinner table in rapt silence, preoccupied on their smart devices—if they even still eat dinner together. Friends have multiple conversations simultaneously through texting and rarely hear each other's voices. Colleagues sit in tightly clustered work spaces, merely feet or floors apart, and prefer to type rather than talk. Surrounded by a multitude of virtual friends, we find ourselves isolated from meaningful relationships. The art of small talk has been lost. And getting to know others deeply through conversation has been replaced by stalking on social media. Awash in a sea of humanity, we find ourselves swimming alone.

I'm not trashing technology. Technology has produced advancements in science and society that previous generations never could have imagined. Technology is simply a tool. And, as a tool, it can be wielded for great good or abused to our own demise. And one of the negative impacts of technology is that, left unchecked, it can actually impede our ability to relate to others in meaningful ways. We must master technology, or it will be our master.

Everyone Is a Free Agent

My father-in-law, Tyrus Acton, worked for the same company for thirty-one years. After his "retirement," he consulted for that company for several more years. He was a traveling salesman. He covered a four-state territory, driving countless miles on interstate highways during the week and was home every weekend. He was a road warrior. He enjoyed what he did and he was good at it. He was committed to the company and the company was committed to him. His appreciation and adulation for the company ran so deep that it impacted the next generation. His son started working for the same company straight out of college and has now been with them for thirty-four years. Today, my brother-in-law, Ty, is the president of Tingue Brown and Company.

My wife, LuAnne, has had a similar career. While she was in college, she met Karlton Jackson, principal of JMG Realty. When he decided to launch his own property management firm to provide services for apartment communities, he invited her to join his team as a leasing agent at one of their sites. That was over thirty years ago. Today, she is the executive vice president of business development and client relations. Although she has had lucrative offers to join other groups, her loyalty remains at JMG. Karlton is like a brother to her and the whole team is like a family. They work hard together—and they play together. They know one another deeply. They are committed to one another, their brand, and their clients. And it shows in everything they do. Loyalty and longevity like this are hard to find in the marketplace today.

Previous generations were told that if they studied hard, were admitted to a good college, and secured high grades, then they could build a career in a reputable company, work their way up the corporate ladder, and eventually retire with a secure pension. That is no longer the case. It's rare to find lifelong careers that span thirty or forty years with the same organization and end with a company-wide celebration and the bestowal of a golden watch.

Today it's common for young people entering the marketplace to have five or six jobs in the first decade of their careers. And people no longer strive for the golden watch. It's a relic of a bygone era. The symbolism of the golden watch, being on your own time in your golden years as opposed to being on the company's time, is no longer relevant. Those entering the marketplace today expect the company to adhere to their time schedule and follow their agenda from the start.

There is very little commitment today in terms of company loyalty. Long gone are the days when organizations could count on long-tenured, faithful employees. Players for life are all but mythical. Today everyone is a free agent.

They play with a certain franchise for a season, however they choose to define a season, and then determine whether they will re-sign with that club or move on to another more appealing proposition. Many variables play into that decision, but the more significant factors are almost always related to the health and depth of their relationships with other team members.

If you want to recruit and retain top talent in today's marketplace environment, then you have to learn how to work as a team and love like a family.

Low-Trust Cultures

Trust is the commodity of leadership. Healthy relationships are built on a solid foundation of trust. Healthy relationships are impossible when there is a lack of trust. When trust is low, resistance is high. People question leadership, push back heavily, and fill communication vacuums with negative assumptions. They are skeptical and suspicious of the motivations of others. Unnecessary friction slows endeavors significantly, if not stalling them altogether.

Conversely, when trust is high, resistance is low. When trust is high, collaboration thrives because people believe the best in one another and reach consensus more quickly. Productive organizations seek to build high-trust relationships across every level throughout the enterprise.

The most critical relationships are those between team leaders and their direct reports. It has been well established that people do not quit companies; they quit managers. The relationship between manager and team member is likely the most important bond determining retention of talent for any organization. The quality of this relationship is paramount. The challenge comes in the fact that few organizations invest adequately to prepare people for leadership. Those who have been successful individual contributors are often moved into positions in which they are responsible for giving oversight to a team, without being equipped to address the relational dynamics. Because they have been productive as individuals, it's assumed that they possess the necessary competencies and emotional intelligence to lead others. This is a faulty and sometimes costly assumption. When companies choose not to invest heavily in growing leaders, it's a clear signal that the organization has little long-term commitment to talent.

It's absolutely imperative that organizations invest in the next generation of leaders, developing bench strength to adequately prepare for the sustainability and growth of the enterprise. The secret is to invest heavily in these high-potential players in such a way that they could go anywhere and be successful, while showing them so much love they would never want to leave.

> **The secret is to invest heavily in these high-potential players in such a way that they could go anywhere and be successful, while showing them so much love they would never want to leave.**

Another factor that has seriously eroded trust in many organizations is the frequency of seeing senior leaders take care of themselves financially with blatant disregard of the cost to others. Many proverbial "golden parachutes" have been constructed for top-tier leaders by ripping apart the fabric of an organization and stitching it together with the threadbare heartstrings of those who have invested heavily at great personal cost. This doesn't have to happen often for people to become cynical. When self-preservation becomes evident among leaders, the desire of others to follow them is greatly diminished. Leaders would do well to remember that the fastest way to success is to ensure the success of others.

Clearing the Undergrowth

Each of these destructive factors must be addressed before we can build a work environment that inspires people to bring their best every day. Like kudzu growing unchecked along a tree-lined country road, these factors are the undergrowth that can choke the life out of any organization's culture. Once the damaging underbrush has been exposed, we can clear it out and begin to nurture the growth of healthy relationships.

>> **GAINING TRACTION:** Questions for Consideration & Application

1. What are a few ways that myopia can creep into leadership?

2. What are the pros and cons of leveraging competition to garner results?

3. How does your organization view its people?

4. How can process efficiency make the work environment less personal? What can be done to counteract this?

5. What elements contribute to a growing sense of isolation in the workplace?

6. Why is trust often called the commodity of leadership?

FOUR

THE CULTURE CONVERSATION

There is nothing more excruciatingly painful than feeling trapped in a life that you've drifted into.

—Michaela Alexis

Wherever people gather, you will have a culture. Organizations have a culture. Teams have a culture. The gym where you work out and the church that you attend have cultures. The philanthropic group with which you volunteer your time and energy has a culture. You even have a culture in your home. Culture can simply be defined as the collective expression of the values, beliefs, and behaviors that individuals bring to any endeavor. It's the manifestation of communal priorities and how people choose to relate to one another. Simply stated, it is how we play in the sandbox with one another. Culture is the single most important differentiating factor of any organization. It has often been said that culture eats strategy for breakfast. And I would wholeheartedly agree. Just as it does for lunch, dinner, and a bedtime snack as well. Products can be reverse engineered and then reassembled. Processes can be imitated and duplicated. But culture goes well beyond what you have or even what you do. It's the essence, the very heart and soul, of any enterprise. It's the true character of any organization. And it must be intentionally crafted with great care and commitment.

The intentional cultivation of a compelling culture should be leadership's highest priority. Since every organization has a culture, the real question is this: Will that culture be by design or by default? Leaders must intentionally and carefully craft a culture by design, keeping a constant eye on the health and well-being of

> **Simply stated, culture is how we play in the sandbox with one another.**

the people and relationships across the enterprise. Thriving organizations have cultures in which authenticity and trust are foundational. Additionally, a sense of deep connectedness and high accountability permeate the ranks. In these environments, people are inspired to bring their best to work every day. Leaders are both champions for and keepers of a strong and healthy culture. They make culture their top priority.

If leaders do not make culture their highest priority, then it can easily slide sideways. It's all too easy to get busy in the details of the business. Putting out fires, addressing initiatives, and simply being buried in the weeds of spreadsheets and agendas, a leader can easily become consumed with the day-to-day operations and lose sight of the importance of building healthy, vibrant relationships. When this happens, leaders may find they have allowed their teams to drift into a culture by default. They may likely wake up one day to find that they neither like where they are nor what they are experiencing from the people around them. This can happen both professionally and personally. Let me illustrate.

I think it's safe to say that we have all been impacted to some degree by the prevalence of divorce. Some have had to contend with the life-altering consequences of having gone through a divorce personally. Others may be children of divorce. Still others have friends and family members who have experienced the pain of such a parting. The negative repercussions of divorce have left a wake of heartache in our society.

When it's appropriate and conditions are conducive for candid conversation with a client who has been through divorce, I will sometimes ask, "So, what happened?" Occasionally they have a backstory of trauma, tragedy, or betrayal. More often than not, however, the response is something like, "I don't really know. We just drifted apart from each other. We got busy with careers and kids. We had different interests and commitments. Eventually, we found ourselves moving in different directions like ships passing in the night. And then one morning, we looked across the bed at each other and admitted we didn't like where we were and really didn't care much for each other anymore. So, we decided to go our separate ways."

They simply drifted apart. That is the epitome of a culture by default. Each party can easily become so consumed in their own myopic minutia that they never stop to intentionally reflect on how they each could have created an environment in which their partner was encouraged and empowered to thrive and find deep satisfaction in the relationship. Instead, they both just drifted into mediocrity and eventually found themselves in the morass of the mundane. They neglected the relationship. They became passive. They may have failed to be responsive to each other's needs. They may have failed to take responsibility for their own actions. They may have refused to engage in self-assessment or make the personal changes necessary to continue to grow their character.

Somehow they emotionally disconnected. And, as a result, their passion faded and they lost sight of what was necessary to grow a healthy relationship. And what happens to couples can also happen to corporations. Leaders must be committed to being champions for and keepers of a remarkable culture. They must not become passive when it comes to relational integrity. They must focus on and fight for cultivating healthy relationships. Otherwise they may very well wake up one day and not particularly care for their surroundings.

If we are going to be leaders who get this culture piece right, then we have to possess a crystal-clear picture of the kind of culture we aspire to craft. I would suggest that a compelling culture consists of a trilogy of characteristics. Singularly, they are significant. Collectively, they produce a cord of commitment that cannot easily be broken. And they build on one another to provide a rock-solid foundation for any endeavor. Simply stated, a remarkable culture is a place where people:

Believe the best *in* one another,
Want the best *for* one another, and
Expect the best *from* one another.

Believing the Best in One Another

Believing the best in one another speaks to trust, which is foundational for all human interaction. Without trust, there can be no healthy relationships. It's virtually impossible to work collaboratively with someone you don't trust. When trust is high, resistance is low. Therefore, change and progress can come quickly. However, when trust is low, resistance is high. In such environments, change and progress come slowly, if they come at all.

When there is lack of trust, skepticism and confusion abound. People question one another and are slow to throw their support behind initiatives led by those whom they hold suspect. Motives are muddled and endeavors never harness the power that could have been generated by a unified workforce. Projects drag and conflicts abound as people posture and self-promote in overly politicized environments. Cynicism rules the ranks. Meetings drag on with debate. People are guarded and seek to protect themselves, fearing the fallout of an admitted failure. They can neither be candid nor bold for fear of retaliation from those in power. These symptoms and more begin to surface when trust is low among a team.

However, when high levels of trust are present, collaboration is enhanced. People who believe the best in one another give one another the benefit of the doubt. They assume the best rather than expecting the worst. This kind of trust is forged through authenticity, transparency, and crystal-clear communication. Teams are positive and productive. They know there is power in being like-hearted, even if they aren't like-minded. They embrace diversity and sharpen one another's thinking. They can disagree without dishonoring one another. And, when they reach consensus, everyone throws their full support behind the endeavor. They harbor no passive-aggressive hidden hope that others will fail. Instead, they share resources and best practices, seeking to ensure the success of each endeavor. The power of rewards and recognition are leveraged for a job well done. And they celebrate frequently. They see failures as learning opportunities and welcome them as simply part of an innovative environment. Transparency and authenticity are cherished, not only as a means to greater interpersonal connectivity but also as vitally necessary for growth and development to occur.

Emotional intelligence—the ability to both read and lead oneself effectively that is at the heart of self-mastery and the foundation for being able to lead others—is cultivated in high-trust environments. Self-awareness and authenticity are cornerstones of emotional intelligence. Authenticity carries with it the ability to know, own, and be responsible for one's feelings, thoughts, and actions. It also includes the capacity and self-confidence to be candid. The phrase "What you see is what you get" comes to mind. When someone is authentic, they don't have to pretend, protect, or self-promote. They feel comfortable in their own skin and both own their actions and take responsibility for the results.

Transparency—the willingness to be known by others—is another powerful hallmark of a high-trust environment. It's speaking and living the truth. It is living in reality. Edwin Friedman expressed it well when he said, "In any situation, the person who can most accurately describe reality without laying blame will emerge as the leader, whether designated or not."[1] The reason is that reality will eventually show up. It always does. And when it does, those who are acting most in alignment with reality will garner respect and emerge as the leaders.

When people pursue authenticity and transparency, clarity abounds. Add the capacity to accurately define reality, and you have the ingredients to create environments in which trust is elevated.

It's also worth noting that like two sides of the same coin, there are also two sides to trust. On the one side, trust has to be earned—it is received when someone has proven themselves trustworthy. Demonstrating character, competence, and connection establishes a sense of trustworthiness. Character is manifested in doing what is right. Competence is shown when someone delivers results consistently, applying the appropriate knowledge and skill. And deep emotional connections are forged through compassion, care, and relating effectively with others.

On the other side, trust must also be given. There must be a disposition and willingness to delegate responsibilities to others, even if they have not yet fully demonstrated their trustworthiness or may have failed in the past. Here, quite frankly, is where many leaders falter. Leaders who have been burned in the past tend to take the path of least resistance and only delegate to those they are confident can carry the load. While this may garner the desired result, it does not provide an opportunity for people to grow their competencies or leadership capabilities. This approach to delegation takes a short-term view. It may garner desired results immediately but fails to adequately prepare people for long-term productivity. Delegation, when used effectively, should be seen as the primary pathway to the development of team members. The purpose of delegation is to grow others, not merely to get more done.

Assignments, when appropriately entrusted to others, can become the most effective means of gaining bench strength. At the same time, lack of appropriate delegation for growth creates a fear-based culture in which poor performance often creates long-term career consequences.

> **Delegation, when used effectively, should be seen as the primary pathway to the development of team members.**

In some organizations, failure is actually seen as fatal, conscripting those poor souls who miss the mark to lesser responsibilities. But strong leaders use delegation wisely and embrace the fact that failure is simply part of the growth process. They do not allow their egos to become too tightly tied to the immediate results. They know that healthy growth and crafting a compelling and collaborative culture are long-term plays. So, they provide a safe environment in which lessons can be learned from failure and then applied to help elevate the performance of individuals and teams. These leaders actually see failure as an investment in the future. They know that very often the greatest breakthroughs come on the heels of failure. And great leaders leverage every lesson learned to hone an innovative and inspirational environment. They allow failure to move them and their teams toward maturity. They don't withhold trust when there are setbacks.

So, believing the best in one another speaks to trust. Trust must be both earned and given. And, when trust is high, change and progress can come quickly and innovation can flourish. Relationships thrive in high-trust environments.

Trust, then, is a litmus test of an inspirational culture.

Wanting the Best for One Another

When working with executive teams, I often ask, "What do you want from your people?" The response is swift and clear. They want results. They want their team members to act responsibly and deliver consistent performance, moving the numbers upward. They usually include some statements about taking care of customers with stellar service and treating others well. But it always comes back to delivering results. Nothing is wrong with that response. I get it. They are charged as senior leaders to grow the company and that translates into driving revenue in the right direction.

But then I follow up by saying, "All right. I know what you want *from* your people. Now, what do you want *for* your people?" The question is usually followed by a long and awkward silence. For most, it's the first time they have ever considered the question. Eventually someone will say something like, "I want my folks to be fulfilled and satisfied in their work." That's a great response on the surface. But when I ask, "What does that mean?" or "How will you know if they are?" I receive another prolonged pause, usually accompanied by a blank stare.

Most employers and team leaders have never really stopped to think about what they want *for* their people. They have well-crafted job descriptions, in which the roles and responsibilities have been clearly spelled out. They have quotas and metrics to measure performance. They have spreadsheets, reviews, and performance improvement plans to make sure each person is clear on the objectives and expectations. But there is often little inspiration.

Before you can inspire others to follow, you must make it clear to those you lead that you have their best interest at heart. And before you can have their best interest at heart, you have to know them deeply. You have to know their joys and dreams. You have to know their passions, strengths, and interests. You have to know their challenges and struggles. You have to be familiar with those forces outside of the work environment that impact the work experience. Do you know their families? Do you understand their backgrounds? Do you consider their hopes and aspirations for the future? The better you know them, the better you can lead them. To put it another way, you cannot lead those you do not love. And you cannot truly love people until you know them deeply and are ready to respond to them personally. When you know people deeply, you can inspire them and tap into their passions and strengths to help them find meaning and fulfillment in their work. The art of leadership is to connect each person's unique giftedness to corporate objectives in a meaningful way.

> **The art of leadership is to connect each person's unique giftedness to corporate objectives in a meaningful way.**

Speaking of meaningful activity, let's explore celebrating success. If you want to inspire elevated performance, you need to know that a one-size-fits-all rewards and recognition program is rarely satisfying. If you're still doling out plaques and awards made of cut glass, please know that the impact is short-lived. I'm not suggesting you deep-six your annual awards banquet. Just be aware that impersonal memorabilia and momentary applause will never garner the same response as a well-thought-out gift or deeply personal gesture.

My wife has taught me this throughout the years. While LuAnne is always gracious in receiving gifts at Christmas and on special occasions, the ones she cherishes the most are those from the heart—the memory book filled with photos of special occasions and notes of appreciation; the special trips organized around activities and places that hold sentimental value; the homemade gifts that require extra energy and creativity; and the carefully crafted card with a handwritten message. These are the gifts she values the most and keeps in her treasure chest of memories. These are far more meaningful than purchases of convenience.

Likewise, when recognizing stellar performance or expressing appreciation for a job well done, try to imagine what would be most meaningful for the recipient. The more personal the reward, the more impact it will have. A gift certificate to take a spouse to dinner at a restaurant that holds sentimental value for that couple or a weekend getaway to a special resort may garner more appreciation than a monetary reward three times the value. Tickets to the family's favorite sporting event or artist's concert will be appreciated far more than a Visa gift card. By thinking beyond simply the award and seeking to discover what would be most meaningful, you are expressing your desire to fulfill that person's dreams and a willingness to do whatever you can to help them craft a better life. It's about wanting the best *for* them. Tap into a person's passion and interests, even when acknowledging performance, and you will be letting them know you have their best interest at heart.

At the same time, when it comes to work, remember that healthy people want to make a difference in the world. We are wired with a desire to make a significant contribution to a worthy cause. The more leaders are able to match up a person's natural talent and passion with work that makes a difference in the world, the higher their level of personal fulfillment and commitment. When leaders do this effectively, they don't have to light a fire *underneath* people, because a fire has already been lit *within* them to do what they are naturally wired to do.

But you cannot lead your people effectively unless you know and love them deeply and want the best for them. So, I will ask you, "What do you want *for* your people?"

Expecting the Best from One Another

The third element of our cultural trilogy is expecting the best from one another. This speaks to responsibility and accountability. Once we have established a high level of trust by believing the best *in one another*, then we have to connect deeply by wanting the best *for one another*. When those two foundational building blocks of culture are in place, we can effectively hold people accountable and expect the best *from one another*. It's critical that each element is stacked in this order. To expect the best from others, before you believe the best in them and want the best for them, will derail your best results. To make demands on others before expressing your trust in and heart for them can easily backfire. If people feel as though they are being pressured to produce before they understand the purpose of their activity and how it connects with their strengths and passions, they can easily feel used.

They may begin to believe they are dispensable. They might even get the impression they are nothing more than cogs in a wheel, grinding out results for someone else's benefit. And no one likes to feel as if they are being leveraged merely for someone else's promotion and self-aggrandizement. Inspirational leaders never lose sight of the fact that people work with them, not for them.

> **❯ Inspirational leaders never lose sight of the fact that people work with them, not for them.**

If we create an atmosphere of high trust and are deeply connected, expressing compassion for those in our care, then we can effectively call out the best that each team member has to offer. When our team members know we have their best interest at heart and we want to empower them to expand their roles and responsibilities, we can coach them to higher performance and hold them accountable for producing the desired results.

One hallmark of a good leader is the ability to clearly connect personal passion with corporate objectives. When people have the opportunity to leverage their strengths and passions to solve problems, they feel empowered to make a difference in meaningful ways. When they see that the value they create is directly connected to the purpose of the organization, they are motivated to do good work. Aligning an individual's strengths with the purpose of the organization can be a powerful motivational force.

Good leaders seek to activate people's natural desire to make a difference and provide opportunities for personal growth. Coaching, encouraging, and even challenging team members to bring their best efforts to the table, inspirational leaders will leverage each individual's desire for self-mastery as motivation to accelerate performance. Healthy people want to get better at what they do, to grow in their knowledge and skill sets. They want to master a level of proficiency and feel productive. They have a deep desire to grow their sense of self-worth, which is enhanced by a conviction that they have made a significant contribution to a worthy cause.

When these elements are in order, accountability simply falls into place. Expecting the best from one another becomes a foregone conclusion. When you want the best for someone, you will not allow that person to settle for anything less than their best. Sometimes that involves being a cheerleader or a coach or a disciplinarian. At other times it involves being a counselor, guiding a person toward a better path. But in each case, it involves calling out the best that each person has to offer.

Expecting people to act responsibly and holding them accountable for the results allows others to have a sense of ownership for their work. If you empower them with the authority to accomplish the objectives and entrust them with the resources to make it happen, then you have essentially demonstrated your trust in them to get the work done. And ownership empowers people to take responsibility for creating value.

Bringing It Together

People ask three questions when evaluating leaders. When these three questions are answered in the affirmative, team members are much more likely to offer their heartfelt allegiance without reservation.

1. *Do I trust this person?*
    As we have said, trust is foundational for any relationship. It's based primarily on the character of the person.

Can this person be trusted to do what is right? Or, when push comes to shove, will they likely demonstrate a lapse in judgment brought about by self-interest?

People who can be trusted create safe environments in which people are treated well and offered respect. Even in the absence of routine, there is a comfortable level of predictability about how the person will respond to a variety of situations, based on that person's values. Emotional volatility is at a minimum. In a word, there is stability.

2. *Do I respect this person?*

This question speaks to competence. Does the person know what they are doing? Do they have the knowledge and skills that produce confidence in those who are following them?

Dependability is the degree to which others can count on someone. Does this person follow through? Do they persevere through difficulties and challenges or quit at the first signs of resistance? Do they see assignments through to completion? And do they complete them with a view toward quality outcomes and relational integrity? If these questions can be answered in the affirmative, then the leader is credible.

3. *Does this person have my best interest at heart?*

Stability is gained through trust, and credibility produces respect. Both play a crucial role in building a strong culture. But the most important element is connectivity. Does the leader know me and are they concerned about my well-being? This is where the situation gets personal. Does this person understand me and can I relate to them?

While trust and respect are essential, the more personally we are vested in a relationship, the more impactful it becomes. The most important question people ask of their leaders is this: Do they truly care about me? Caring for someone implies taking care of that person. That is not to suggest that the leader can always influence factors to guarantee a positive outcome. In fact, in some situations, they shouldn't. But the fact remains that the more deeply a leader knows their team members individually, the better they can serve them personally. And the more they demonstrate care and compassion, the more comfortable their team members will feel with their leadership. Even when hard decisions have to be made, leaders who have established deeper relationships will often be given latitude by those they lead.

Trust engenders stability.

Competence creates credibility.

Care and compassion produce connectivity.

And where stability, credibility, and connectivity are present, there is almost always an increase in productivity. Depth of relationship is almost always inversely correlated with heightened performance.

>> **GAINING TRACTION: Questions for Consideration & Application**

1. How would you define *culture*?

2. Why is culture the single most important differentiating factor of any organization?

3. What three elements constitute a remarkable culture and why is each important?

4. If the art of leadership is connecting personal passion to corporate objectives, then how do you effectively do that?

5. What are some ways in which you can recognize and reward your team members in a more personal way?

6. What are the three questions people ask about their leaders? How do you think your team members would respond in evaluating your leadership?

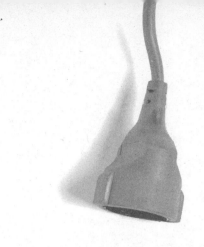

STAY IN THE FRAY:
HUMILITY

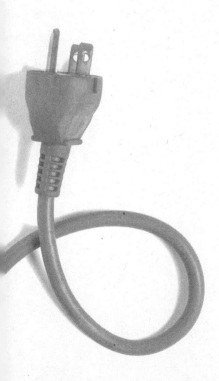

FIVE

NOBODY IS NORMAL

The only person you are destined to become is the person you decide to be.

—Ralph Waldo Emerson

In Mel Brooks's classic comedy *Young Frankenstein*, Gene Wilder plays the part of Dr. Frederick Frankenstein, the infamous creator of the towering, tap-dancing, "cultured and sophisticated man about town." In one of my favorite scenes in the movie, the good doctor questions Igor on the origin of the freshly implanted and somewhat suspect brain.

"Now, that brain that you gave me, was it Hans Delbruck's?"

"No," replies Igor.

"Ah, good! Would you mind telling me whose brain I did put in?"

"And you won't be angry?"

"I will not be angry," the doctor states emphatically.

"Abby someone."

"Abby someone? Abby who?" Dr. Frankenstein continues to probe.

"Abby Normal."

"Abi-normal?"

"I'm almost sure that was the name," Igor responds gleefully.

"Ha, ha, ha." The doctor rises to his feet and places his hands around Igor's throat. "Are you saying that I put an abnormal brain into a seven-and-a-half-foot-long, fifty-four-inch-wide gorilla? Is that what you're telling me?"[1] And with that question wafting in the air, the good doctor throttles Igor and bounces him up and down as his eyes begin to bulge out.

This hilarious scene serves as the setup for what turns out to be a comedic rendition of a fanciful tale that is a parody of its more serious telling. As funny as this scene may be, leaders sometimes feel as if they are dealing with *Abby Normal* people when confronted by a myriad of interpersonal challenges and unhealthy behaviors manifested among those whom they oversee. Juvenile attitudes, passive-aggressive activity, disingenuous conversations, and basic disrespect can be collaboration killers. Unhealthy relational dynamics can wreak havoc among teams, rendering members frustrated and unable to focus on the work at hand.

While it may seem appropriate and even convenient at times to label challenging individuals as abnormal, I caution against relegating people to any category. Doing so may hinder leaders from dealing directly with difficult individuals and issues head on. There is no *normal* when it comes to relationships. Or, said another way, every individual is unique. *Normal* is defined as "approximately average in any psychological trait, as intelligence, personality, or emotional adjustment; free from mental disorder; sane."[2] While it may be statistically possible to find the mean when it comes to rational intelligence testing scores, it's considerably more difficult to ascertain the same when it comes to personality or even emotional adjustment. And, from my experience, it's safe to say that the vast majority of people truly believe themselves to be above average. So, we have a perception problem and a whole host of leadership problems when we begin to pronounce others as *not normal*.

The reality is that we are all broken to some degree or another. There is no normal. Even the sharpest people you know, who seem to have it all together when you first meet them, are most certainly struggling with something on some level that renders them somewhat less than they desire to be. What I am trying to say is that everybody seems normal until you have the opportunity to observe more closely. Inevitably, we all begin to show cracks in our character when scrutinized.

Rather than writing off others as being less than normal, a better approach to leadership would be to grow in our empathy and authenticity.

Humility Breeds Authenticity

Humility is the character quality most often associated with servant leadership. As much as humility is talked about in leadership circles, it's still widely misunderstood. Some see humility as meekness or being mild-mannered. Some would

81

suggest that it's the antithesis of arrogance or pride. Others may use platitudes, such as "Humility isn't thinking less of yourself; it's thinking of yourself less." While each of these may shed some light on this important character quality, humility remains hard to define and even harder to achieve.

At its core, humility is the ability to see oneself honestly, without pretense. Humility involves a clear acknowledgment of the frailty of humanity and the recognition of our own brokenness. The paradox is that we cannot change ourselves until we accept ourselves just as we are. We must be comfortable with the awareness that we are not perfect and have no need to posture ourselves as being perfect. We can be honest with others and ourselves as we embrace our strengths and work to enhance those aspects of ourselves that could potentially limit our leadership. Simply stated, we can be authentic. We do not need to pretend to be something we are not.

Good leaders are okay with the fact that they are a work in progress. They are comfortable in their own skin, no matter how freckled with failure it may be. They are confident in their abilities and quick to share their shortcomings. They are not embarrassed by the truth that they are not an expert on every subject. As a matter of fact, people who possess humility can genuinely celebrate the strengths of others without letting it threaten their own sense of self.

> **Good leaders are okay with the fact that they are a work in progress. They are comfortable in their own skin, no matter how freckled with failure it may be.**

A leader who is able to see their own weaknesses or shortcomings, and acknowledge them freely, is inspirational. A leader who has no need to pretend to be the smartest person in the room can harness the talent of others who may be able to complement and strengthen their endeavors. The ability to recognize and leverage the strengths of each person creates a collaborative environment in which creativity flows freely and collective intelligence is leveraged effectively.

The converse is also true. A lack of authenticity leads to incapacity. Think of the insecure executive who is constantly struggling to prove themselves to others. Every meeting has the potential to become a battleground, where emotional sparring wastes precious time. Such a leader uses power plays to keep others in their "rightful place." When insecurity is in the ranks, collaboration is curtailed. Lack of trust often leads to command-and-control structures, in which positional power replaces relational influence.

Not long ago, I was retained to consult in a corporate environment like this. The leader was a decent man with a strong strategic bent. He was actually brilliant. Many of his ideas were well-thought-out and had the potential to be significantly impactful. But there was an elephant in the room—his inability to gain substantive buy-in from the senior leadership team. At the heart of the problem was his need to constantly prove he was *large and in charge*. While many described him as charismatic and kind, those who worked closely with him knew better.

The character flaws he concealed in the calm became clearly evident when he experienced pushback or pressure. Those who knew him well saw the worst. Frequently, meetings were initiated with a series of leading questions. It would quickly become apparent to those in attendance that the purpose of these gatherings was not for brainstorming and problem-solving. The agenda was clearly set and the conclusions all but foregone when everyone took their seats at the table. Rather than expanding the possible options with wide-ranging solutions, the scope quickly narrowed to those ideas he wanted to have rubber-stamped. Pushing back or questioning his direction was seen as insubordination. He was threatened by anyone or anything that might raise doubt as to whether he was the smartest person present.

What was even more interesting was his reaction when I pointed out that he was actually the problem. Unable to embrace the feedback, he began to call into question my ability to ascertain the true nature of the issues at play. In other words, he attempted to assassinate me as the messenger. Apparently, he had brought me in to "fix" everyone else. Unable to accurately analyze his own thoughts, feelings, and motivations, he started casting aspersions on me and everyone else who he felt was potentially blocking his path. I was released of my responsibilities as advisor and within six months, all but one of his senior team members had found somewhere else to invest their time and energy. I'm sure he saw it as clearing the house of opposition, but the company hasn't grown since. As a matter of fact, it's in a slow and steady death spiral.

Leaders like this are hard to follow. While they seek to prop up their image at all cost, they undermine their own credibility with those whom they lead. Everyone knows they don't single-handedly hold the keys to the kingdom. Yet they delude themselves into believing that, in order to garner respect, they have to exert their authority. Interestingly, just the opposite is true.

A single leader cannot be good at everything. Smart leaders know their limitations and intentionally surround themselves with folks who are more intelligent and more competent than they are. Then they lean into those gifted individuals for their expertise and experience. They are not easily threatened. Quite the contrary, they are quick to admit what they don't know, and cannot do well, in order to enlist the support of those who have more to offer. This allows others to not only own the process but also be accountable for the results. It also creates much deeper engagement and, consequently, buy-in throughout the process. Synergy is created and greater value is offered when everyone is able to leverage their strengths and passion to produce collectively more than could ever have been created through the mere stacking of individual contributions.

Authenticity is the ability to quickly claim and utilize your unique gifts and strengths without falling prey to false humility. It also means that someone can even more quickly acknowledge those areas in which they have no passion, knowledge, or expertise. Simply put, an authentic person can be real. At the same time, authenticity allows good leaders to quickly admit when they have been wrong and apologize. They also seek reconciliation in order to restore broken relationships, when appropriate.

So, humility is the ability to deal effectively with one's own humanity. Humility breeds authenticity. And authenticity produces empathy.

Authenticity Produces Empathy

If authenticity is accepting our own humanity, then empathy is accepting and connecting with the humanity of one another. The more effectively we have dealt with our own humanity, the more we relate to others in a spirit of grace. It's a reality that the harder we are on ourselves, the more likely we are to be hard on others. And the flaws that bother us most in someone else may be the very issues we need to address in ourselves. In psychological terms, this is called *projection*, which is the tendency to ascribe to someone else one's own attitudes, feelings, or suppositions as an unconscious defense against anxiety or guilt. It's highly likely that the areas in which we tend to be judgmental of others are the very areas in which we ourselves need to grow. Before we cast aspersions on others, we would be wise to be introspective enough to ascertain whether we first need to deal with some personal character defect.

Maturity includes the ability to embrace our own frailty while allowing ourselves the grace to grow. Empathy involves loving and leading others while understanding their brokenness and encouraging them to pursue their own growth.

Empathy is the degree to which we are able to connect emotionally with others, without condescension and judgment. Empathy is the ability to feel what another feels and understand a situation from the perspective of another by placing ourselves in their shoes. Empathy helps us suspend judgment until we thoroughly understand the situation and have a chance to investigate the dynamics at play. When a decision is rendered, empathy allows for compassion even when delivering difficult news. Empathy does not mean we avoid making the hard calls. Rather, empathy provides us

> **Empathy is the degree to which we are able to connect emotionally with others, without condescension and judgment.**

86

with the connectedness to deliver challenging news in a compassionate way.

The more we can embrace our own frailty and get in touch with our own emotions, the more likely we are to connect with others in their humanity. While character and competence produce trust in a relationship, empathy produces a deeper emotional connection. When a relationship is marked by a high degree of trust and empathy, it's likely to weather even stormy seasons because each person respects the other one.

Dealing with Brokenness

Can we just admit that we are all broken? None of us is everything that we desire to be. We all have room to grow. Healthy individuals constantly seek to grow. And, as has been stated, relationships provide the context within which we can grow and cultivate character. The challenge comes in that most organizations are so focused on short-term productivity that they don't invest in the long-term development and success of their people—and they do so to their own peril.

Teflon's nonstick properties make it a wonderful thing to have on a skillet when you are scrambling eggs. But it is not a good descriptor of a healthy organizational culture. In a "Teflon Culture," people don't stick. They seem to slide right off the grid, especially after an apparent failure. Teflon leaders are impervious to blame or criticism. They don't assume responsibility when things slide sideways. They prefer to release others of their responsibilities rather than run the risk of a blemished reputation. They won't put their neck on the line for anyone or go to bat for their team members. And those around them know this to be true and operate in fear.

Failure is unacceptable and people are dispensable. Second chances are rare and only offered grudgingly.

However, second chances are often the greatest opportunities leaders have to energize their workforce. When we express belief in and invest in those who have failed, we are making a huge statement and creating an atmosphere conducive for greater commitment. We are saying that we don't throw people away at the first sign of trouble and we are committed to the growth and development of one another, even in the face of setbacks. When we do this, those who have been extended grace feel motivated to right the situation. In healthy people, grace cultivates gratitude. And gratitude is one of the greatest ingredients that bonds people together. When team members experience grace and feel gratitude for it, we don't have to light a fire under them because we will have effectively fanned the flame within them.

Companies that treat people like pawns never experience the full benefit of having teams composed of mature and deeply bonded individuals who believe in one another and feel that others have their best interest at heart. Instead, such companies put a premium on defect-free performance and sacrifice personal development on the altar of perceived perfection. This, of course, is impossible to sustain and breeds an atmosphere of uncertainty. People begin to posture and pretend in order to preserve their appearance. Productivity may peak in the short-term, but it's unsustainable. The culture becomes increasingly impersonal and eventually collapses due to relational undernourishment. There is a revolving door of talent, and replacement costs shoot through the roof. Team satisfaction and customer experience suffer for lack of stability. Eventually, business becomes rote and relationally void. And customer loyalty evaporates like fog on a sunny morning.

But companies that take the risk to restore and invest in the growth of others may very well garner a workforce of people whose loyalty and longevity outpace those who are far more gifted. Discretionary effort and commitment are often the response from those who have been given a second chance. When clear, constructive developmental feedback is offered in an atmosphere of grace, significant growth can occur. And as people bring a better self to the table, better results are almost certain.

Leaders would do well to create work environments that are characterized more by Velcro than they are Teflon. Leaders who take the risk to afford others a second chance may be well served if they offer such grace judiciously. Those who are deserving of additional time and attention may very well advance to become some of your strongest leaders. Second chances may produce the stickiness needed to keep good people on your team. And good leaders, who know how to grow their people, will seize these opportunities and invest accordingly. The secret is knowing in whom you should place such confidence.

> **When clear, constructive developmental feedback is offered in an atmosphere of grace, significant growth can occur.**

Investing in the wrong people can create an atmosphere of enablement, in which bad behavior goes unaddressed. While I challenge every organization not to be overly quick to terminate their talent, sometimes it's necessary to part paths.

Worthy of a Second Chance

The latter part of this book is dedicated to helping leaders by providing some specific tools to hone the workforce. When leaders invest in strengthening the culture of the enterprise by cultivating rich relationships, good things tend to happen. Like breaking up fallow soil before planting the seed, good leaders know how to prepare their teams to produce bumper crops. But to produce *remarkable results*, you first have to have *remarkable people* on your teams.

To be clear, remarkable people are not perfect. None of us are. But certain attitudes and values characterize high-potential players who will make the most of a second chance. When these particular behaviors are present, you can enjoy a high degree of certainty that your investment of time and energy will produce a worthy return. Let me list seven things you should look for when trying to determine whether you should take a risk on someone.

1. *They receive feedback well.*

   Feedback fuels growth. People who want to get better at what they do welcome advice and even criticism, particularly if a trusted coworker or manager offers it. They view such input as an opportunity to reflect on weaknesses they may not see clearly in themselves. Knowing that we all have blind spots, they embrace critiques as gifts and seek to glean insight and apply practices that will make them better. Even when advice is offered from a suspect source, they do not quickly dismiss it. Instead, they search for the kernel of truth that may be buried in the furtive feedback. They know that even one's enemies can become allies in pointing out weaknesses that should be shored up.

Not only do they receive feedback well, but they also actually pursue it. They want to know how they are doing and what they can do to improve. Rather than avoiding feedback because of their insecurities, they thrive on challenging themselves to move beyond their limitations. They are grateful for any insight they may gain that will help them hone their capacity to connect with others in more meaningful ways. This doesn't mean they seek to please everyone. They know better. It's impossible to do that. Those who attempt to please everyone lose both their personal identity and their integrity. Rather, they garner insight from every possible source and then vet it accordingly. Like a gold miner panning for gold, they sift through the silt in search of even the smallest nugget of truth that will make them relationally richer.

Those who get defensive and deflect or project their issues onto others when faced with feedback are probably not worth giving another chance. They would likely squander the opportunity.

2. *They are truthful.*

When confronted with the truth, the employee worth your risk doesn't deny it. No matter how much it hurts or may cost, they are truth-seekers and truth-tellers. They don't spin, hedge, or create an alternate reality. They don't vacillate or waver with the changing winds of popular opinion. They demonstrate a steadfast commitment to speaking forthrightly.

Conversely, those who attempt to confuse others or convolute the issues with deception or misdirection undermine the trust that may have been created through transparency. Attempts to alter reality by spinning the facts will only postpone the inevitable. Sooner or later reality will show up. And when it does, those who stand in the truth will emerge respected for being forthright, even if the facts are not favorable for them.

> **Those who speak and live the truth are typically trustworthy of a do-over.**

Relationships are built on trust. And trust can only be garnered when there is truth. Anything else is simply an illusion that will disappear when the light exposes the lie. Deception must be dealt with seriously as the relationally destructive element that it is. Those who speak and live the truth are typically trustworthy of a do-over.

3. *They own or acknowledge their failures.*

Few things have the capacity to restore favor more quickly than simply acknowledging a failure. While some may try to conceal or deflect responsibility, taking ownership is a mark of maturity. When someone owns a failure, they are welcoming the opportunity to take corrective action.

When someone refuses to own the problem, they will also likely refuse to take corrective action. If it's not their problem to begin with, why should they be forced to clean it up? They claim to not be a part of the problem, and they refuse to be a part of the solution. Therefore, they really have no role to play in creating value. Those who create little value are worthy of little latitude when it comes to evaluating the risk of extending another opportunity.

4. *They take responsibility for making things right.*

Value creators strive to make things better. Even if a dilemma is not of their own doing, they want to make a positive wake in the world. They embrace challenges as opportunities to create value and attempt to use their strengths and passion to solve problems. They are quick to lend a helping hand. They are far less concerned with affixing blame than they are in rectifying wrongs and getting situations righted.

Those who are willing to own the problem and take responsibility for making it right are individuals worthy of your investment of time and energy.

5. *They want to grow.*

As odd as it may seem, not everyone has a desire to grow. Some are more concerned with preserving an image than they are with moving toward maturity. They see self-protection and self-promotion as more important than growth and advancement. This pretense leads to posturing. And posturing precludes self-awareness. Without self-awareness, growth is all but impossible. If someone cannot be challenged to change, then change is not likely to occur until extreme circumstances force the issue by bursting the illusion.

Healthy individuals want to grow. They are willing to be confronted, stretched, and challenged because they have an innate desire to be better. Those who demonstrate a desire to move beyond their present capacity are likely good prospects to become quality performers into whom you can pour your resources.

6. *They are quick to apologize.*

Where pride is present, apologies are few. There is an ancient proverb that says, "Where there is strife, there is pride. But wisdom is found in those who take advice."

Pride leads to strife. An inability to acknowledge one's mistakes and apologize to those impacted is the essence of pride. When someone shows blatant disregard for how their attitudes and actions have impacted the lives of others, they are toxic. And toxic people need to be marginalized. Removing toxic people from an organization can go a long way in building a healthier culture.

Wherever there is constant conflict, there is unhealthy behavior.

7. *They initiate reconciliation.*

Healthy people will take the initiative to make things right with others. They understand the power of and necessity for healthy relationships. When things go wrong, they own their part and work to reestablish the relationship as best they can.

This, however, does not mean owning what is not their responsibility. Taking responsibility for the actions of others leads to enabling bad behavior. For reconciliation to occur, each party must own their part in the problem. Only then is full restoration possible.

If someone is consistently unwilling to own and take responsibility for their part in the problem, then the problem is likely to recur. An excuse is a clear signal that you are going to have to deal with the issue again. People who constantly make excuses are toxic and you will likely have to distance yourself from them.

The main point here is that healthy people seek reconciliation. Whether reconciliation occurs will depend on the actions of both parties. Look for those who are intent on making things right and restoring relationships.

While we need to build organizations with more Velcro and less Teflon, sometimes it's necessary to part ways with unhealthy people to build a strong culture. When that is the case, you are smart to cut ties quickly rather than allow poor behavior to continue to infect the enterprise. Good leaders must ascertain who will get a second chance and who should be given the freedom to move on. Assessing people based on these seven characteristics will help in making that determination.

Ready, Aim, Fire!

When you deem it necessary to relieve a person of their responsibilities, how you do it is critical. It will make a defining statement both to that person and to everyone else on the team.

I had the privilege of working with a leader who had a knack for firing people while maintaining a strong sense of connection. She handled each situation with deep compassion. On more than one occasion, I witnessed individuals approach her in public and fawn all over her. As they walked away, she would often say something like, "That's Kathy. She used to work for me, but I had to fire her. Now she's working over at _____ and doing a great job!"

The first time I witnessed this, I was a bit bemused and dismissed it as an oddity. But the second time, I had to ask how it was possible for her to fire folks in such a way that made them not only genuinely glad to see her again but actually seek her out across a crowded room. She was gracious enough to share her secret with me.

"To lead people effectively, you have to love them deeply," she said. "I love my people. I get to know each team member and their families. I want to know what drives them. I want to understand their hopes, dreams, and aspirations. I also want to know what challenges they face on a daily basis. I want to know what they enjoy away from work. All of this helps me know better how to lead them and how to reward them for a job well done. I truly want the best for them, and I check in on them regularly. I want to know not only what they are doing but how they are doing. Sure, I want to know that they are fulfilling their responsibilities, but I also want to know whether or not they are personally fulfilled in their work. It's important to me that my people enjoy their work and the other people on the team. Because, when you enjoy your work and you like the people you work with, life is just better."

Then I asked her how she handled underperformance. Here is what she said.

"When I see someone underperforming, it's generally because they are either experiencing some challenge in their personal life or they simply are not happy in what they are doing. So, I ask them. I may say something like, 'Hey, I've noticed recently that things have been a bit rocky. You haven't been giving your best at work and I've seen your performance slip. Let's talk.'

"At first they will typically try to project an image that everything is just fine. But shortly into the conversation they will almost always ask me what I have noticed. This is my opportunity to explore a little deeper."

"How do you do that?" I asked.

"I might say something like, 'It doesn't seem to me that you are truly happy in what you are doing. Happy people tend to do what they do well. Your performance recently hasn't led me to believe that you are happy. Are you finding fulfillment in your work?'

"After a little probing," she said, "they almost always confide in me something that has presented them with a challenge. If it's on a personal level, I express empathy and attempt to offer whatever support I can provide, however limited it may be. If, however, it's job related and presents a substantial barrier, then I take the conversation in a different direction.

"I ask, 'What would make you truly happy? If you had a magic wand and could use it to create your ideal job, what would that look like?'

"Sometimes those conversations allow us the opportunity to look across the organization to find a position in which the person's strengths and passion are more aligned with the responsibilities. If a move can leverage their gifts more effectively, then it's a win for that team member and the organization. If there is no apparent match, I may suggest that together we begin to look outside the organization for opportunities that would be more personally fulfilling. If I have connections to another organization that would be a better fit, I gladly agree to make an introduction and offer my recommendation. Should we find a better fit outside the organization, again it's a win for the team member and for the organization because it gives both the opportunity to move forward in a more productive manner. I have acted in the best interest of both parties and it's appreciated."

Her approach is profound. She is keenly aware that happy people do good work. And good leaders want the best for their team members—whether that is with the organization or somewhere else where they are more fulfilled. When people know you genuinely have their best interest at heart, they are more likely to believe the best in leadership. And when these two elements are present: *wanting the best for* and *believing the best in* one another, then you can *expect the best from* one another.

People Are Not Your Greatest Asset

I will often ask a gathering of leaders, "By a show of hands, how many of you truly believe your people are your greatest asset?" Almost every hand in the room quickly shoots toward the ceiling. If you were present, maybe yours would too. We all tend to place a high value on people, at least in terms of lip service. Maybe we do this instinctively. Maybe we are conditioned to respond this way. But the reality is that people *are not* the greatest asset of any organization.

Now, before you slam your book shut in disagreement, please let me explain. Apart from the fact that an *asset* is defined as "an item of ownership having exchange value,"[3] I believe the term itself is derogatory when referring to team members and take exception to it. However, there is another more obvious reason that such a statement is untrue. Even if you prefer to stick with the term *asset*, I think you would still agree with me that the *right people* may very well be your greatest asset, but the *wrong people* are your greatest liability. So, it's not all people, but the *right people*, who bring value to the organization.

As leaders, we must have the wisdom and relational maturity to differentiate between the right people and the wrong people when we are seeking to grow healthy cultures that inspire elevated performance. An inability to do so and make the necessary decision to part company with those whose values do not align with the rest of the team, or the enterprise at large, could prove detrimental to crafting environments in which healthy relationships can be nourished and grown to fruition.

>> GAINING TRACTION: Questions for Consideration & Application

1. How would you define *humility*? Why is it such an important quality for leaders to possess?

2. Authenticity can be a bit unnerving. Does the thought of being authentic with your people make you a bit nervous? Explain your answer.

3. Would you say your culture is more like Teflon or Velcro? Explain your answer.

4. Sometimes it's necessary to move folks out of the organization. When do you know that it's time to help someone make an exit?

5. What can you do to fire someone gracefully?

6. How would you say happiness ties into performance?

SIX

THE GROWTH SPIRAL

> You ain't gonna learn what you don't wanna know.
>
> —Jerry Garcia

G ood feedback is a gift and should be received with gratitude. Feedback fuels growth, providing personal encouragement as well as the insight and perspective we need to pursue the changes that lead to maturity.

We all have room to grow. Feedback shines a light on shortcomings we may not otherwise see. A blind spot could be described as a character deficiency or an area that requires personal growth, about which we have been uninformed. Feedback is invaluable and can provide the mirror that allows us to see what might otherwise remain hidden to us—but most likely not to others.

The challenge, of course, is that feedback is not always easy to receive. We all bask in the light of positive feedback. We need it. We relish affirmation. But feedback that isn't so glowing can be difficult to bear. It bursts our bubble of self-delusion. It exposes us. It hurts because it forces us to see things that we would prefer remain hidden. Or it may scrape the scab off an old wound that we wanted to salve a little longer. Whatever the case, feedback that addresses critical deficiencies isn't pleasant to receive and it isn't easy to deliver effectively either.

We'll deal with the subject of delivering effective feedback in a later chapter. But before we can deliver effective feedback, we must first master the art of receiving feedback well. Receiving feedback requires that we both be deeply in touch with our emotions and have the maturity to harness them.

Every experience in life is emotionally framed. Emotions are wrapped around first impressions. Conversations evoke emotions. Relationships are fraught with emotions. Emotions are the visceral response to life. They can enhance our experiences, but they should never exclusively control our response to those experiences. Like lights on the dashboard of our lives, they give us an indication of how well our internal components are running; they provide inspiration and even information to guide us. But we should seek to master our emotions rather than letting our emotions master us. Of course, this is easier said than done.

At the risk of oversimplifying this complex subject, let me attempt to explain why emotions are so powerful. When we experience anything through our senses, that information is first screened by the reticular activating system (RAS) to determine its level of importance. To prevent sensory data overload, the RAS screens out all information that is deemed peripheral and causes us to focus on only that which is deemed necessary.

When the information is relevant and significant enough to warrant our attention, it passes through the limbic system. Here emotions are attached to the sensory data. Long before our prefrontal cortex has the opportunity to supply rational thought, our emotions come into play in an attempt to define and interpret what we are experiencing. Only after this wash of emotion takes place does the brain's executive functionality kick into gear. If our feelings are strong enough and allowed free rein, our emotions can literally hijack our higher reasoning, enslaving us to impulsive reactions. Obviously this is not optimal and is why some argue that emotions should, at best, be suppressed and that good decision-making be based on reason alone. However, research has proven this assumption to be faulty. Patients who have experienced damage to the amygdala, which is part of the limbic system, find it difficult to impossible to make decisions about even the simplest matters. Thus proving that without emotions, decision-making is impaired.[1]

> **The best decisions are made when reason and emotion are blended, without one dominating the other.**

The best decisions are made when reason and emotion are blended, without one dominating the other. Stoic processing of information can be harmful in that it fails to factor in the impact that emotions provide. Likewise, emotions run amuck can cause us to make disastrous decisions because of limited impulse control. Emotional intelligence requires us to both recognize and define our emotions, and then leverage those emotions to enhance and not dominate our decision-making processes.

So, let me explain how all of this factors into feedback. When we receive feedback, whether solicited or unsolicited, we enter into a spiral. That spiral can either ascend to personal growth and transformation, or it can descend into desperation and alienation. Let's take a look at how both of these occur, beginning with the progression and consequences of not handling feedback well.

Descending the Growth Spiral

When we don't handle feedback well, not only are we unable to benefit from any possible insights for growth that we may have gleaned, we can also complicate the situation further by compromising our credibility in the process. Let's say someone is providing you with feedback. This is what I call a clutch situation.

Think of the clutch on a car. It's designed to help you easily engage the gears so that the power generated by the engine can be transferred to the drivetrain to turn the wheels and produce motion. Relationally, a clutch situation is any circumstance in which two or more individuals need to effectively connect (engage with each other) to produce positive movement in that relationship. A clutch situation could be a performance review, a meeting with a team member, a conversation with your spouse, or a teaching moment with a teenager. It could even be a brief encounter with a stranger. Almost every human interaction could be considered a clutch situation. Every encounter with someone gives us the opportunity to learn something new if we know how to garner feedback, whether spoken or not.

For the sake of this discussion, let's imagine for a moment that the clutch situation is in the form of feedback from a superior or a team member. Whether offered as part of a performance review or a collegial conversation, the individual is extending constructive feedback for improvement. Of course, how that feedback is offered can either tee up that conversation for success or derail it into failure. But right now, I simply want to focus on the response. And the first response we will be looking at is a poor response, causing a downward spiral.

Spiral One: Defensiveness

A critique or criticism can be hard to stomach, no matter how well it's delivered. We are all prone to have a negative emotional reaction to what we perceive as criticism. And that negative emotion causes warning signals to go off and defense mechanisms to be erected. This natural impulse to get defensive triggers a downward spiral that can have devastating consequences. Once defenses have been engaged, a pattern typically follows, rendering the clutch situation void of any positive impact. For once the defenses are up, the slippery spiral descends to the second level.

Spiral Two: Rationalization

While rationalization is an appeal to reason, it's usually an attempt to minimize consequences by ascribing causes for poor conduct that superficially seem reasonable but are actually unrelated and not creditable. In other words, rationalization is an attempt to make excuses or justify bad behavior. It's an effort to deflect responsibility or explain away culpability.

But excuses never correct the problem. It has been said that an excuse is simply a promise you make to yourself that you will have to deal with the issue again. Excuses simply postpone the inevitable. Despite our efforts to rationalize our behavior, sooner or later the issue will surface again. When we refuse to receive and assess difficult feedback, we are prone to repeat poor patterns.

Rationalization—the antithesis of authenticity—disengages the gears of growth and impedes relational development. Rather than facing reality, smoke and mirrors distort or redirect our attention away from the primary focus. This inability to look at oneself honestly, and the subsequent lack of ownership, will eventually cause the situation to degenerate to the next tier in the downward spiral.

Spiral Three: Stagnation

As the situation degenerates, a lack of engagement between the parties involved prevents them from relating effectively or connecting deeply with one another. The emotional barriers erected through rationalization to protect delicate egos are the same barriers that prevent us from authentically connecting with others.

When we rationalize, we are essentially saying we are not open to considering whatever is being presented that may challenge us to grow. This unwillingness to consider our shortcomings causes us to get stuck in a rut, where there is no opportunity for personal growth. We bunker in and justify our position. We may shift the blame to others or even attack the messenger. Whatever the reaction, we dig in our heels and refuse to budge from our bunker. The other person, depending on their disposition, may do the same thing. If they feel dismissed or attacked, things are likely to escalate. At this point, one or both parties may attempt to blow the other out of their respective bunkers.

Before long, the issue spirals out of control. Emotions escalate and both parties are on edge. Whether they continue to engage in verbal bombardment or retreat, there is now a rupture in the relationship. If one chooses to remain aggressive, the other may go passive. But don't take the sudden withdrawal as a sign of acquiescence. More likely, it's simply an attempt to dodge the shrapnel, not an indication that the issue is resolved. Unresolved feelings can go underground and continue to mount until there is a volcanic eruption.

Neither is fighting fire with fire helpful. Both parties only get incinerated. Ultimately, what happens in these fiery engagements is that the relationship follows a continual descent to the fourth level of the spiral, with its accompanying consequences.

Spiral Four: Alienation

Whether the third tier in this descent produces a standoff or a fiery exchange, the result is the same. Both parties are at odds with each other. Those who first became defensive and attempted to rationalize their behavior are now most likely resorting to desperate measures to prop up what is left of their shattered egos. These responses can span the spectrum, from simple awkward attempts to reframe the conversation to all-out attempts to undermine the credibility of the other party through subversive activity.

Without resolution, a separation between the two parties involved is certain. This emotional distancing causes alienation between those who need to connect in order to create value and positive relational movement. Alienation fosters desperation. People begin to act out of self-interest rather than seek what is mutually beneficial. Immaturity, rather than growth, prevails. This downward spiral all begins when an individual seeks to self-protect and self-promote rather than create value for oneself and the other person. Without candor and authenticity, growth is preempted by value extraction and posturing.

Ascending the Growth Spiral

The alternative to descending the Growth Spiral is to approach each clutch situation as a value creator. The question then becomes, How can I leverage this opportunity to produce the greatest value for everyone involved? This includes looking deeply at oneself and seeking to bring a better self to every endeavor. This attitude of openness creates an upward spiral of growth that can become inspirational. Let's take the same scenario and talk about how we can ascend in this situation and engage the gears for growth.

> **› Change is inevitable. We can either grow through feedback and increased self-awareness, or we will be forced to change through crises.**

Change is inevitable. We can either grow through feedback and increased self-awareness, or we will be forced to change through crises. Unfortunately, most people never change until it's forced on them. They rock along, set in their ways and defending their positions, until calamity hits. That may come in the form of a pink slip, a Dear John letter, or an unwelcomed doctor's diagnosis. Whatever the case, change that is forced on us is often seen as a hardship. When change is defined as such, most will attempt to endure the hardship and resist the change. However, when we receive feedback as a gift and seek to apply the insights we have learned, we can often make the changes necessary to avert crisis and move toward relational maturity. When we move in the direction of maturity, we are ascending the growth spiral. Like the downward spiral, the upward spiral also has cycles. Let's look at each of these cycles to see how we can get into growth gear and move toward maturity.

Spiral One: Openness

When given feedback, we can either choose to embrace or resist it. Mature individuals grow more mature through the feedback of others. Good feedback allows us to see what may have remained hidden to us. We can then address these blind spots as part of our overall character development. This feedback may also give us insight as to how to more effectively relate to others. Either way, feedback received well can build a stronger relational bridge between two parties.

It all begins with a person's willingness to listen intently without becoming defensive. Even if the comment or feedback is not coming from someone with the purest motives or the messenger struggles with the delivery, those who are open can always find a kernel of truth in what is said. This openness creates an atmosphere of honesty and authenticity, where issues can be explored for the mutual benefit of those involved.

Spiral Two: Honest Evaluation

When someone chooses to embrace feedback, it becomes an opportunity to seek and apply new truths. And truth applied leads to transformation. But embracing feedback first requires humility, which allows us to see ourselves honestly, without pretense, and leads us to greater self-awareness. Humility is an acknowledgment of our humanity, the awareness that we are not perfect and have no need to present ourselves as being perfect. We all have room to grow. Unfortunately, many people are stunted in their growth because they are self-deluded, believing things about themselves that simply are not true. Rather than embracing change, they resist and try to present themselves in a flattering light.

Self-awareness comes through honest introspection and evaluation. A healthy evaluation of a situation causes us to see ourselves as we truly are and to weigh the options and potential outcomes of our actions. It forces us to stop and consider the factors involved. Candid evaluation launches us on a journey to seek truth. But the extent to which we find truth is directly proportionate to our openness and willingness to receive it.

When we embrace feedback without hedging, spinning, or deflecting, we can consider its implications and adjust accordingly. To shift significantly may require enlisting the help and support of others. This is when we have the opportunity to considerably strengthen our relational bonds. It could be impactful to solicit the support and encouragement of the very one offering the difficult feedback.

After acknowledging where growth needs to occur, we could benefit by asking the messenger to serve on our *personal development board*. Ask for that person's involvement in holding us accountable, providing needed resources, or offering encouragement when they recognize positive movement on our part. After all, they were concerned enough to bring something to our attention in the first place. Enlisting their assistance allows them to continue to stay engaged in the process. It also makes a statement about our seriousness to make a change. Remember, relationship catalyzes growth. And strengthening the relationship by asking them to continue to offer insight and feedback can accelerate growth, both personally and relationally.

Spiral Three: Solution Orientation

When we ask someone to stay engaged, we are essentially asking that person to help us come up with solutions. Rather than getting bogged down in debating the details and bunkering into stagnation, we are moving beyond focusing on the problem and heading toward a solution.

Shifting into a solution-oriented mind-set is a pivot point. It takes the spotlight off the negative aspects and their repercussions and begins to redirect the conversation and energy toward finding solutions. When we humble ourselves and ask the other person to help us resolve the issue, we allow them to connect with us on a deeper level. If our offer is accepted, that person now joins our team and is on our side, helping us rectify the issue. Together, we move toward relational maturity.

Spiral Four: Inspiration through Unity

Rather than attacking one another, which often happens in the spiral of descent, we are united in addressing the issue. We are in the foxhole together rather than in opposing bunkers. We address the concerns together as allies rather than waging war on one another. We can actually ask that person to have our back by offering us continual feedback to ensure that the corrective actions we've taken remain on course. That person can provide another set of eyes and ears to help us monitor whether progress is being made. When one demonstrates this depth of humility and sincerely invites another to offer assistance, it does wonders in creating a spirit of unity. And unity is a powerful force that can be leveraged for greater good.

> **Unity is inspirational; it turns doubters into dedicated supporters.**

While divisiveness is destructive, unity is inspirational; it turns doubters into dedicated supporters. When we approach challenging circumstances with relational maturity and a commitment to move beyond the problem, even dire situations can have inspirational outcomes.

You will also discover that the more open you are to receiving feedback from others, the more likely they will be to receive feedback from you when the tables are turned.

One Last Word on Feedback

Receiving feedback well requires substantial intestinal fortitude and emotional stability, particularly if it's delivered in a less-than-desirable way. But demonstrating the emotional intelligence to embrace and honestly assess all feedback is a sign of maturity. Growth personally and relationally is the payoff. And if you really want to up your game, then don't wait for feedback to come your way. Ask for it.

Many organizations go to great lengths to utilize a variety of instruments to give leaders insight for personal growth and development. For example, 360-degree reports are designed to provide thought-provoking feedback from those within a leader's sphere of influence. Gathering feedback from direct reports, colleagues, and superiors, these formats consume a tremendous amount of time, energy, and resources to produce information to help individuals grow in their leadership capacity. Lengthy questionnaires are completed by a host of individuals, data is compiled, reports are generated, and then information is interpreted and delivered by an objective third party. All this is done to provide helpful information to enhance growth personally and professionally.

Do you see the irony of it all? We have manufactured artificial forums to overcome relational deficiencies. We have gone to great lengths to systematize a process for giving feedback because most organizations are filled with people who are so relationally immature that they don't know how to effectively relate to one another. Wouldn't it make sense to instead challenge people to grow up and move toward authenticity and relational connectedness?

Let me offer an alternative. It's what I like to call the *Poor Man's 360*. It's a single question that can provide a wealth of developmental feedback. I'm not sure of its origin and I do not claim it as my own, but it's one I use frequently with significant people in my relational realm. To set it up, choose those who are closest to you and give them carte blanche to be completely candid. In fact, tell them you want them to offer you the last 10 percent—the difficult feedback that most are afraid to express.

The first 50 to 70 percent of feedback is typically positive and contains a lot of fluff. The next 20 to 40 percent is usually thought-provoking insight that challenges us to grow. But the last 10 percent of feedback is the hard stuff. The stuff that exposes the ugly and unsightly cracks in our character. It's what we don't want to hear but desperately need to hear. It's the raw, real conversation that has to take place in order to move toward relational maturity. Give them the freedom to go there with you. Then ask them the following question: What's it like for *you* to be on the other side of *me*?

Meaning, how do you experience me? What do you see in me that I may not see in myself? In what areas do I need to grow to bring a better self to life? On what do I need to work in order to become a better leader, spouse, parent, or friend? Please give me the gift of your feedback.

I have discovered that those who are courageous enough to ask this question are the most self-aware individuals I know. They have discovered the benefit of asking this question of those closest to them. And they ask it frequently.

I am a dad. I have three sons and a daughter. I know pretty well how to rear boys. They're easy. You have quality time together, wrestle with them frequently and feed them occasionally. You tell a boy you love him by putting him in a headlock or roughhousing. I made it a priority to volunteer my time to coach almost every team Ryan, Colton, and Jonathan played on until they were each in high school. But being a good father to my daughter, Lindsay, was quite another story. It was more of a challenge for me to participate in the pretend tea parties. It was difficult for me to wholeheartedly engage in helping her select dresses for her dolls. Without my wife, I am not sure I could have survived the emotional roller-coaster ride of adolescence, with all its inherent drama. Don't get me wrong. Lindsay is now a beautiful young lady who is making her mark on the world and I could not be more proud of her. But I didn't always know how to connect with her emotionally.

So, to stay connected with her heart, we would do daddy-daughter dates on a regular basis. We would go to dinner, or a movie, or just hang out together at a park. Sometimes she would accompany me on trips as I spoke to various groups across the country. Intentionally, our conversations would often include the Poor Man's 360 question. I would say something like, "Hey, Linds, I need to know something. How am I doing? I mean, what's it like for you to have me as your father? You know that I don't always do this dad-daughter thing well. From your standpoint, what can I do to be a better father for you?"

I cannot overstate how much that single question, and her answers in response, has made me a better parent and a better person. The same is true when I ask that question of LuAnne. I become a better spouse. But let me warn you. Before you ask the question, you better be emotionally prepared for the response. Some of the feedback may surprise you. It may be painful to hear. It may even challenge your integrity. But if you are willing to embrace it without getting defensive, you may find that those closest to you can offer a clearer window into your very soul. And if you can take their feedback to heart and solicit their help, then you can make the changes necessary to enhance your relationships.

In conclusion, healthy relationship catalyzes growth. And feedback fuels growth. Those who learn how to receive feedback well demonstrate greater self-awareness and become relationally richer. Those who actively seek feedback become richer still.

›› GAINING TRACTION: Questions for Consideration & Application

1. Why is it common for people to get defensive when receiving feedback?

2. Reflect on a time when you descended the Growth Spiral. Describe the situation and the outcome.

3. Now contemplate how that same situation could have been different had you worked to ascend the Growth Spiral. What could you have done differently?

4. Why is feedback so important to personal growth?

5. What can you do to prevent your emotions from hijacking your reasoning?

6. What are some artificial forums that have been created in corporate circles to overcome relational deficiencies?

7. Why is the Poor Man's 360 such a powerful question?

SEVEN

FACE VALUE

What we achieve inwardly will change outer reality.

—Plutarch

What we experience outwardly is merely a reflection of what we have or have not mastered inwardly. The term *emotional intelligence* has become a popular way of expressing a relational reality. The better someone monitors and manages one's own emotional energy, the better they can master their emotions and leverage them for their personal benefit. And the better one can read and lead through their own emotions, the better equipped they are at reading the emotions of others and leveraging them to lead effectively. It has been substantially proven that those who demonstrate higher levels of emotional intelligence consistently outperform their counterparts with greater rational intelligence. Said another way, those who are relationally savvy and emotionally stable often outpace those who are technically smarter.[1]

The ability to master one's inner world of emotions is indeed a powerful thing. When we harness our emotions constructively, we are better able to lead others effectively. The converse is also true. Those who are unable to manage their emotions productively often create toxic environments for those who must live with the fallout. Many otherwise productive work environments have been rendered incapacitated by a single individual who simply could not rein in their emotions. These ticking time bombs can go off, sometimes without warning, spewing relational shrapnel that sends everyone ducking for cover.

> **Leaders who create safe environments will find that their teams work collaboratively and productively.**

Leaders who create safe environments will find that their teams work collaboratively and productively. Safe environments result when leaders demonstrate emotional maturity and craft a culture in which sweeps of the workplace are done regularly to find and deactivate these dangerous relational land mines before they are detonated.

Leadership Goes Boom

John was a sales manager for a midsized medical device company. As the economic winds became adverse, the pressure mounted for his team to hit their sales numbers. As he experienced pressure from those above him to drive the numbers north, his inability to manage his internal turmoil became evident to everyone on his team. Meetings were filled with threats and innuendo. Dictates were given with little discussion or problem-solving. Team members, who once demonstrated patience, soon became irritable with one another, and the folks in operations suffered under John's scrutiny when challenges arose that slowed the sales process.

A spirit of fear and mistrust started to permeate the ranks. An atmosphere of cooperation and collaboration was replaced by a CYA (Cover Your Assets) mentality. Morale and performance began to wane. Eventually, people found other opportunities and began to depart through the back door. Those who had no other option continued to show up physically but were emotionally absent. John had single-handedly created a toxic environment that was killing his people. He was leaving mangled morale in his wake, and lifeless bodies were washing ashore.

After spending a little time with John and his team, I could see clearly that he lacked both the skill and the will to delve into the depths of his own psyche to unearth the issues locked deep within his soul. Historically, he had been a high performer. By all accounts, he was prone to occasional bouts of volatility. As long as things were running smoothly, he provided helpful leads and support for his team members. But the minute his reputation was threatened or tarnished by anything less than a stellar performance from his team, he addressed it as a personal assault.

If anyone spoke poorly of him or attempted to give him anything other than affirmation in their feedback, he saw them as disloyal and they were immediately "targeted" for punitive measures. Sometimes that meant he simply avoided the perpetrator and withheld support or resources. On other occasions, he would lash out verbally at the perceived traitor. Because the office atmosphere prevented authenticity and candor, the negative thoughts and feelings of team members were forced underground, where they continued to build pressure. Gossip at the watercooler was an ever-increasing problem. Those involved in less-than-complimentary conversation would scatter like roaches exposed by the light whenever John would walk down the hall.

And John's problems went well beyond the work environment. During our second session together, he received a phone call from his wife. After a brief exchange, he hung up on her and was visibly agitated. He then explained that the two were in marital crisis and discussing divorce. From his perspective, she was being demanding and totally unreasonable. On top of all the pressure at work, he didn't have time to deal with her "hormonal hysteria," as he called it. Then he began to recount in vivid detail several recent situations that supported his claim that she was losing her sanity. He was deflecting and projecting.

I seized the moment and made a bold statement. "Maybe her hormonal hysteria, as you call it, is the greatest gift you could ever be given," I said. He sat there in stunned silence as he tried to absorb the statement. He was dumbfounded. He literally didn't know how to process what I had said. After a long, awkward silence, I continued.

"Look, I'm going to be candid. Things are bad with the team. We probably disagree as to why, but we both know that to be true and there's not much time to turn this around. That's why I'm here. But, more importantly, that's why your wife is here."

"What do you mean?" he asked. "She knows nothing about the business!"

"That may very well be true, but she knows you. And she may know you even better than you know yourself. You see, I've discovered that I can tell what kind of a man a husband is by looking at the face of his wife. If her countenance is radiant and she carries herself with an air of confidence, then I can tell you that almost without exception her husband has created a loving, safe, and affirming environment for her at home. If, however, she is either combative or downtrodden and despondent, very often I have found a man who is oblivious to the needs of his wife and extracts more value from her than he gives to her. Of course, there are exceptions, but I find that more often than not the wife is a reflection of the man. You can often tell the heart of a man by looking at the face of his wife. I guess you could say that your spouse is a walking billboard extolling your personal brand. So, what kind of message is that billboard sending to the world?"

John immediately became defensive. He began to list all the reasons why he should be nominated for Husband of the Year. Then he went back to enumerate stories that illustrated why living with her was so difficult. I sat patiently until he paused to take a breath. When he did, I simply responded by saying, "Bovine excrement!"

Now, I don't normally speak that bluntly, but his defense mechanisms were so well crafted and his bunker dug so deeply that my only recourse was to try to blast him out with bluntness. For a moment I thought he was going to leap across his desk and throw me out of his office. His face turned red and the veins in his neck began to bulge. He tried to stare a hole right through me. But I didn't flinch in maintaining eye contact. It was a momentary standoff. Finally, he drew a long breath and sat back a little in his chair, his eyes still fixed on mine. And then he said, "What do you mean that you can tell the heart of a man by looking at the face of his wife?" His question gave me the opportunity to explain.

Creating or Extracting Value

My wife has an emotional bank account. Every day, and in every encounter, I will either make a deposit into that bank account or take a withdrawal out of it. If I seek in each situation to create value for her, then I'm making deposits. If I take care of her physically and emotionally, then I'm making deposits. If I seek and honor her opinions, then I'm making deposits. When I serve her, I'm making deposits. When I'm more concerned about her happiness than my own, I'm making deposits. When I listen with empathy, I'm making deposits. When I affirm her, I'm making deposits. When I provide a safe place to discuss heartfelt issues, I'm making deposits. And the more deposits I make into her emotional bank account, the richer our relationship will become.

However, if I expect more from her than I give to her, then I'm making withdrawals. If I put my needs above hers, then I'm making withdrawals. If I make demands of her, without counting the cost, then I'm taking withdrawals. Whenever I put myself first, I'm making withdrawals. And if I extract more through my withdrawals than I give with my deposits, then it won't be long until our relationship is emotionally bankrupt. Or think of it as a relational reservoir. The more I pour into the reservoir, the more our relationship is going to be well watered. But the moment I begin to drain the reservoir, our relationship becomes drier.

Every day, and in each encounter, we can choose to be either a value creator or a value extractor. Value creators leverage every situation as an opportunity to bring more to the table than they take away. They look to make life better for others. As we create value for others, those relationships become richer over time. It doesn't matter whether in the office or the home, the same principle applies.

The greatest challenge to any relationship is when one or both parties enter into it with the idea of extracting value. You see this a lot at networking gatherings. People show up and size up. They evaluate everyone according to what value they think the other person can offer to their endeavors. Folks mix and mingle with the objective of making connections that will facilitate their agendas. Have you ever been on the receiving end of an exchange at such a gathering in which you didn't measure up to someone's predetermined profile? It's actually laughable how quickly the conversation can turn and how rudely you can be dismissed when a value extractor loses interest in your story. These meetings are often replete with desperate people and egregious egos, each pushing to promote or protect something. People are focused on what they can get *from* you while giving little thought to what they might be able to offer *to* you. Everyone goes through the formality of exchanging business cards, but then most quickly cull through them to discard those that have little or no potential of fulfilling their self-promoting purposes.

Value creators, however, are more likely to be involved in NetWeaving. My friend Bob Littell, founder of NetWeaving International, defines NetWeaving as a "Golden Rule" and

"Pay It Forward" form of networking. NetWeaving involves thinking more about how one can create value by connecting others who share a common interest or may be able to serve one another in a mutually beneficial manner. It's about promoting someone else's story above one's own. It's an understanding that all the good things we desire in life are the by-product of creating value for others. It's focusing more on how we can create value for others rather than trying to prove to others how valuable we are. It's not about attempting to extract value for oneself. Rather, it's a constant awareness that in each encounter we may very well be able to bring something to the table or make an introduction that could bring immense value to someone else. In doing so, we can make a positive impact in someone's world. We can make someone's story better. We can create value. And the more value we create for others, the more invaluable we become.[2]

The same principle holds true in our closest relationships. Meaning and fulfillment in life are found in value creation, despite how society often romanticizes value extraction. You see this warped perspective in a thousand subtle ways every day.

Jerry Maguire is on my short list of favorite movies. A cutthroat sports agent who seemingly has a moral epiphany and finds love in the process makes for a great story. The movie has several memorable lines, including "Show me the money!" and "Help me help you!" But the movie contains two other lines that are emotionally impactful. They are delivered in a scene in which Jerry (Tom Cruise) is explaining to Dorothy (Renee Zellweger) what happened the previous evening in what proved to be a turning point for their fledgling company. At the end of the scene, she utters the words that have caused many macho men to get misty-eyed: "You had me at hello." Prior to that, Jerry makes a heartfelt declaration: "You complete me!" This simple three-word line has been known to make women swoon. The scene is oh, so romantic. Break out the tissues, right?

Not so fast! The screeching sound you just heard in your head was my stepping on the brakes.

Let's analyze this. The whole scene isn't romantic. It's sick. It's not about value creation; it's about value extraction. Rewind the reel. Let's take a look at what Jerry actually says just before he delivers the famous line that tugs at our heartstrings.

He says, "Our little project, our company, had a very big night . . . a very, very big night. But it wasn't complete. It wasn't nearly close to being in the same vicinity as complete, because *I* couldn't share it with you. *I* couldn't hear your voice. Or laugh about it with you. *I* miss my wife [long pause for effect]. We live in a cynical world—a cynical world. And we work in a business of tough competitors [another long pause so you can reach for the tissues]. *I* love you. You . . . complete *me!*"[3] Cue the tear ducts.

If you go back and read the lines again, in which I added italics for emphasis, who is the focal point of his comments? How many times does *I* come up? Who is this really about? It's about him! Now, admittedly, he does say, "I love you." But then he immediately follows it up with "*You* . . . complete"— whom? *Me!* In the final analysis, it's still about him. It always was and still is about him. And that one line compounds the corruption of our thinking about relationships.

You see, most people think someone will magically come into their life who possesses everything necessary to fill the void they feel in the depths of their soul. We look for someone to satiate the longings of our hearts. To make us feel good about ourselves . . . to *complete us*. It's the myth of a "soul mate." Some believe that, in a perfect world, there is a perfect match for them and once they find that person and join their lives together, they will experience bliss everlasting. But this thinking does not reflect reality.

If you buy into this bogus belief, then there is a logical progression to your approach in finding a mate. You begin your search for someone who can give you what you need to feel good about yourself. Do you see the focus here? It's a value-extraction mentality. When you do find someone who seems to make you happy and appears to have, at least temporarily, filled some of the gaps in your character (e.g., you succeed in holding the ugly parts of you back long enough to get to the commitment phase of the relationship), you take the leap. Sometime after the honeymoon, however, you begin to once again be faced with the reality of your frailty. You get frustrated or angry because your needs are not being adequately met. You feel lonely. You begin to experience the same longings you had before marriage. So, you blame your spouse for the shortcomings in the relationship. Or, worse yet, you assume you made a horrible mistake in marrying the one person who you thought could complete you. And although married, you continue to search for such a mythical mate, guaranteeing that you live in misery.

The world is filled with broken people in search of someone to fill the deficits in their own character and make them feel complete. But when two people who are both attempting to extract value from each other enter into a relationship, it's akin to two leeches latching onto one another and sucking the lifeblood out of one another. That is a pathetic, yet accurate, analogy of many marriages. In a value extraction–focused marriage, each person ends up drained and dying. The lifeblood is literally sucked out of the relationship.

But here is the reality. Every holy union is composed of two unholy, broken people. For a marriage to thrive, a value-creation mentality is required on the part of both spouses. When I focus on what I can bring to the relationship, as opposed to what I can get from it, I become a value creator and attempt to construct an atmosphere in which each person can flourish. I seek to bring the best of who I am to the table and constantly look to provide emotional and physical support to ensure my partner has everything I can provide to encourage their growth. I am not responsible for compensating for their shortcomings or concealing their character flaws. Rather, I am to live with this person in authenticity and transparency, loving them unconditionally and leading by example to the very best of my ability. I give without any expectation of reciprocity. I give because it's the right thing to do. If that person is of the same value-creation mentality, then our relationship grows and becomes a blessing to us both and to others. When I bring my best and the other person brings their best, we complement, not complete, one another.

A good marriage is a work of art crafted over the course of time by two broken people who recognize their frailty and extend grace to each other. They love each other through their brokenness and create value for each other, even in seasons when it might not be returned. It's a commitment that is made steadfast by a *we*, as opposed to *me*, mentality. This type of relationship places an emphasis on *us* instead of *I* and encourages each person to constantly look out for the best interest of the other.

You can tell by a woman's countenance whether her husband is a value creator or a value extractor. And, by the way, the reverse is also true. A man whose wife is a value creator is a happy man indeed. It's often easy to detect those who are in a relationship that is sucking them dry. I would also dare say that you determine much about the character of a leader by looking at the faces of those on their team. Show me a flourishing team and it's almost certainly led by a value creator. These leaders know that true success comes from doing everything within their power to ensure the success of those they lead. They know happiness and fulfillment come through working hard to provide happiness and fulfillment for others. They know the good things we desire in life are by-products of creating true value for others.

> **A good marriage is a work of art crafted over the course of time by two broken people who recognize their frailty and extend grace to each other.**

What Does Your Spouse's Face Say?

I turned to John and asked, "So, what does your wife's face say about you?" He was frozen in silence. He didn't have to respond to the question. We both knew the answer.

I broke the silence. "Now, it's remotely possible that your wife is as bad as you say that she is and there may be some mental health issue at play. But at one point you saw so much in her that you thought you couldn't live without her. So, what has changed? Is it that she is mentally unstable, or is it likely that you have both been looking to one another to get your needs met rather than focusing on how you could meet each other's needs? Is it possible that you are merely like the rest of humanity in that you are both broken people looking for love? And when you don't get the love you think you need and deserve, you begin to dictate and demand that your needs be met before you seek to meet one another's needs? Could it be that your emotional baggage is banging up against her emotional baggage and bruising you both?"

"I do love her," he responded in a softer voice. "Truth be told, I am afraid of losing her. She just makes me so crazy that I can't control myself. She is unfair and unreasonable. And when she begins to attack my character, I feel like I am going to explode," he said, the tension coming back into his voice.

"But what if she's not really attacking your character?"

"You obviously haven't heard our conversations," he retorted.

"True. But right now it sounds like she is desperately trying to get something from you. Would you say that is correct?"

"Of course, she wants my money!" he said with a grin, bringing a little levity into the conversation.

"And if things continue on the current course, she may very likely get it," I jested in return. "But seriously, what do you think she is trying to get from you emotionally?"

"I suppose she's looking for love," he offered.

"I would agree," I said. "But what does love look like to her? What does she need? Have you ever asked her?"

"I've never asked her that question."

"Well, maybe you could. Maybe you could ask her what she really needs from you. In my experience, people usually know what they need to find fulfillment in a relationship. If she responds, and if you listen intently without rebuttal, you might have a good place to start in restoring the relationship. And if you focus on becoming a value creator and doing your best to provide her with what she says she needs, it might begin to change the tone and temperature of the relationship."

"And what if she doesn't reciprocate?" he questioned.

"Well, if you're doing your part in order to get a particular response from her, then you're not really focused on being a value creator. If you're offering value only to receive something in return, then you're a poser. You're only pretending to be a value creator while actually attempting to manipulate the situation as a value extractor. A value creator gives with no expectation of anything in return. They give because that's just what they do."

"But what if things don't change for the better?" he continued.

"They very well may not, at least not at first. It's going to take some time. You didn't get here overnight and it won't be fixed overnight. But if you remain steadfast in your desire to be a value creator and learn how to receive her feedback, then I have every confidence that things will begin to shift for the better. The toxicity of value extraction was injected into your relationship with your wife a long time ago, and it has caused both of your hearts to atrophy. The only cure is value creation. If you regularly ask for her feedback on how you are doing and sincerely focus your efforts to provide what she needs emotionally, I think you will begin to see a change in her attitude. But be patient. It may take some time."

What Does Your Team Need from You?

If you've never asked your team members what they need from you, maybe you could.

It's a simple question.

Good leaders want to know how they can serve their teams better. They don't guess or speculate. They ask. Sometimes the expectations are irrational or difficult to meet. In those cases, good leaders know how to reset the expectations. Often asking the question can lead to new ways in which the leader can facilitate a healthier team dynamic or remove barriers that are obstructing stellar performance. Sometimes they cannot solve a problem, but they can provide a listening ear or an empathetic response that lets another person know they have their best interest at heart.

If you want to be successful, then focus on making everyone around you successful and your success will be guaranteed. If you want to be happy, then focus on making those around you happy by creating value for them and your happiness will follow. I can tell you from personal experience that I am the happiest as a spouse when my wife is happy. A happy wife makes for a happy life! I am happiest as a parent when my children are doing

> **Good leaders want to know how they can serve their teams better. They don't guess or speculate. They ask.**

well and are happy. And I am happiest as a team leader when my team members are finding happiness and fulfillment in their work. But I won't know if they are happy, or what I can do to make the atmosphere more conducive for healthy relationships, if I don't ask.

Leaders who ask their team members specifically what support they need in order to excel typically demonstrate a depth of character and emotional maturity. Those who respond as value creators know how to cultivate stable relationships and tend to have happier teams. And you can tell a lot about the character of a leader by looking at the faces of their team members.

Let's Face It

Months passed. I stayed engaged with John and his team. Our coaching time together was equally distributed between fostering a more collaborative and inspiring work environment and attempting to save his marriage. He worked tirelessly on both fronts. And what he discovered in the process was that the same approach he was using to mend his wife's heart also worked with his team. In a very real sense, the lessons he was learning at home he was able to apply in the marketplace. His wife was essentially becoming his most valuable business coach. And she knew absolutely nothing about the business. But she knew a lot about him and what he needed to do to foster healthy relationships.

The more he leaned into his wife and listened to her with a commitment to change himself and become a value creator, the more effectively he began to relate to his team members. Rather than posturing and protecting, he began moving differently in his world. He welcomed feedback. In fact, he asked for it. And he took to heart what he heard and made a conscientious effort to move in more positive ways.

When the holiday season rolled around, the office threw a party. John's wife came for the celebration. It was the first time anyone could remember her ever attending. But there she was at his side. Shortly after the festivities began, John came over and introduced me to his wife, Susan.

"I'm so happy to finally meet you," she said, beaming with a smile that put the lights on the Christmas tree to shame. "John has told me so much about you and your work with the team. I just have to say thank you for all you have done for John. You have truly made a difference in our world."

"Well, thank you for your kind words, but John is the one who has done all the work," I responded. "And it's truly a pleasure to meet you. I have to tell you that I love your smile. You know, I can tell a lot about the character of a man by looking at the face of his wife. And from what I can see, you have a good man at your side!"

As they excused themselves and began to walk away, I grabbed John's arm and whispered in his ear, "That's a very impressive billboard!"

He smiled.

›› GAINING TRACTION: Questions for Consideration & Application

1. Define emotional intelligence and discuss why it's so important in leadership.

2. What are the substantial differences between networking and NetWeaving?

3. What does the countenance of your spouse say about the nature of your relationship?

4. What would you say your team members need from you as their leader?

5. Purposefully ask each one of them what they need from you and compare it to the list you created. What differences and similarities do you see?

EIGHT

FEAR FACTOR

Too many of us are not living our dreams because we are living our fears.

—Les Brown

n 1892, among Stanford University's pioneer class was a student who was struggling to pay his tuition. His father had died in 1880, when he was six years old, and his mother had passed away only three years later, leaving him an orphan with little resources and no family to support him in his academic endeavors. In an effort to raise the funds necessary to continue his education, he and a friend decided to host a musical concert on campus. They discovered that Ignacy J. Paderewski, the world-renowned Polish pianist, was planning a tour in the United States, and so they reached out to his manager to see if he would consider adding a stop to his itinerary. Paderewski's manager required a guarantee of $2,000 for the performance and a deal was struck.

The boys worked hard to make the concert a success. But by the time of the scheduled performance, they had fallen woefully short in raising the funds through ticket sales to cover the guarantee. Following the concert, the boys gave Paderewski and his manager the $1,600 they had managed to raise and a personal pledge to make good on the shortfall as soon as they were able to secure the additional funds. When Paderewski heard their plight and the purpose for which the performance had been scheduled, he tore up the contract and returned all the funds to the two young men, instructing them to use the money instead to pay the expenses of the concert and to apply the rest to their educational fees and tuition.

Paderewski went on to become the prime minister and then foreign minister of Poland. When the First World War ravaged Poland, it left more than 1.5 million people starving in its bloody wake. The country's newly formed government had no resources with which to buy food. Desperate to help his people, Paderewski reached out to the US Food and Relief Administration for assistance. Established by Woodrow Wilson and under the direction of Herbert Hoover, the agency was responsible for the administration of the allies' food reserves. On receiving Paderewski's request, Hoover agreed to help and launched one of the largest relief operations ever mounted in Europe. He quickly shipped tons of food grains to feed the starving people of Poland, sustaining them until the next year's crops could be planted and harvested.

Paderewski traveled to Paris to thank Hoover personally for the aid he had provided for his nation and countrymen.

As Paderewski began to thank him for his assistance, Hoover interrupted him and said, "You shouldn't be thanking me, Mr. Prime Minister. I am the one who should be thanking you. You may not remember this, but several years ago you gave a concert in Palo Alto, California. The young men who organized the concert could not afford to pay what the contract required from the ticket sales. You generously forgave them the debt and helped two students work their way through college. I, sir, was one of those young men."[1]

Herbert Hoover went on to become the thirty-first president of the United States. During World War II, Hoover led the Commission for Polish Relief, which assisted hundreds of thousands of Poles. And in 1946, he once again visited Poland to draft another plan that would aid Poles for the next three decades. Hoover's long relationship with Paderewski and the Polish people started with a simple act of kindness, demonstrated by an individual who could never have fathomed the impact of such a gesture. Yet it changed the course of an entire nation's history.[2]

There are essentially two types of people in the world—value creators and value extractors. Value extractors position themselves in every situation to extract as much value for themselves as they possibly can, with very little or no concern for how their actions may impact those around them. They are the takers of the world. They live with a *scarcity mentality* that operates on the assumption that there isn't enough to go around. So, in order to survive, they believe they must get to the table first and secure as much as they can for themselves. Value extractors live for themselves.

Value creators, however, constantly seek to bring as much value to the table for others as they possibly can. They live with an *abundance mentality* based on the belief that if we work collaboratively, then together we can create more collectively than we ever could individually. And the value created together can then be shared among those responsible for creating that value. Value creators live to enhance the lives of others. They live selflessly. But, in living selflessly, they greatly enhance their own existence.

Value creators bring their best to the table daily for the benefit of everyone they encounter. They don't do it to gain something in return. They do it because it's the right thing to do. They do it simply because it's who they are. Sometimes they see that good reciprocated in tangible ways. Sometimes they don't see the results at all. But they know that doing good for others is a good thing to do and so they do good because it aligns with their values.

Paderewski was a value creator. He created value as he wrote and performed music that moved the masses. He created value as a philanthropist who gave his time, energy, and resources to a variety of humanitarian efforts. He created value as a national leader and diplomat as he worked to restore a devastated Poland in the aftermath of war. And he created value for individuals he encountered, as he did with young Herbert Hoover. He didn't create value for notoriety or personal gain. He did it because that was who he was. It was his nature. Creating value was consistent with his values. And it shaped his legacy.

Living in Fear

Healthy individuals have a deep desire to do good. Something within the human spirit is stirred when we see others impacted through acts of kindness. We feel a sense of fulfillment when we have the opportunity to make someone else's story just a little better. Most people want to be part of something larger than self that makes a positive difference in the world. We long to leave a legacy. When we die, we want to leave more behind than merely material possessions that will gather dust and rust. The idea of value creation resonates with those who are seeking to build strong relationships. Yet many of us falter and fail in applying the principles and employing the practices necessary to create value because we are stunted by fear.

Fear is the great robber of relational richness. We fear disapproval. We fear placing ourselves in a position in which we could potentially be hurt. We fear disappointment. We fear rejection. We fear being taken advantage of by others. We fear offending. We fear there may be a lack of reciprocity. We fear not measuring up. We fear being exposed as inadequate. We fear many things, and that fear prevents us from moving relationally toward others in bold ways that could truly make a lasting positive difference in their lives. So, it might be helpful if we confront a couple of these fears. Since fear works best in darkness, shining a little light on the subject may be just the key to dispelling some of the lies and misconceptions. Let's analyze a couple of fears that many folks wrestle with when calculating the cost of becoming a value creator.

> **❯ Fear is the great robber of relational richness.**

Others Might Take Advantage of Me

What if others take advantage of me? Let me answer this question simply. Some will. Expect it.

It's a common concern. The question may induce some caution, but it should not deter us.

Although healthy people are wired to create value, many experience a problem with their circuitry. The problem is selfishness. Selfishness short-circuits valucentricity—the alignment of values. While many people talk about creating value, adding value, or bringing value to their endeavors, very few actually know how. Most, believing they are creating value, are actually merely positioning themselves to extract value. Think of the consummate sales professional who gives the appearance of sacrificially going above and beyond to secure a sale. If he truly is making the offer with no strings attached, then such a gesture would fall into the category of value creation. However, if he is doing so only to establish a "chip," which he intends to cash in when the customer gets to financing, then he is simply "giving to get," as the tired sales saying goes. That would be nothing more than manipulation with value extraction as the ulterior motive.

The prevalence of selfishness and self-promotion makes many people vulnerable prey to a *me-first mentality*. A me-first mentality breeds self-protection and a myopic orientation, causing value extractors to walk through life oblivious of others. Focused on "getting what's theirs," these value extractors are wolves in sheep's clothing, waiting to feed on the goodness of others. And they do. And they will. Sooner or later you will encounter someone who will take your generosity and then expect more, without offering anything in return to you or to others. Don't be surprised when it happens. If you practice value creation, it will inevitably happen to you.

But fear of being taken advantage of is no reason to cease creating value for others. Value creation is life-giving. Value creation is inspirational. It is, in a word, transformational. When we mark someone's life for the better or do something that somehow improves another person's story, we have made a difference in that person's life. We have truly made a positive wake in the world. We have made the world a better place. We have brightened the beacon of humanity.

Will there be those who, for various reasons, take advantage of our kindness? Yes. But fear of such folks should not deter us from following our own value construct. Even if our gesture of goodwill is not appreciated, we can still relish the fact that we followed our conviction to be a value creator. The litmus test in determining what one should do is not whether the gesture will be reciprocated. The value creator follows the inclination to move away from being a consumer of value and toward being a contributor. A tree is known by its fruit and not by the character of those who consume its fruit. A tree must stay true to what it's destined to produce. A good tree produces good fruit.

When value creators connect with other value creators, movements of good are easily spawned. People's lives are improved and their communities are strengthened. People are inspired to collaborate and relationships become that much richer. When a community of value creators comes together, value extractors are easily identified because they stand in stark contrast to everyone else. When value extractors attempt to coexist with value creators, they are quickly and effectively marginalized. Their true colors eventually shine through and they are seen for what they really are: self-centered.

My Needs Might Not Be Met

What if my needs aren't met? This is a legitimate question. We all have the need to be loved and to feel we belong. We have hopes, dreams, and aspirations. We have a desire to be appreciated and respected when we give of ourselves to others. So, the question becomes, What if I focus on meeting the needs of others and my own needs go unmet? While it's possible that a value creator's needs may go unmet, it's very unlikely. While there is no guarantee it will work, the approach one needs to take to ensure one's own needs are met is completely counterintuitive.

You may remember the name Abraham Maslow from your psychology 101 course in college. Maslow's famous *hierarchy of needs* was first set forth in 1943 in a paper titled "A Theory of Human Motivation." Taking a radically different approach to his work, in light of other contemporary psychological studies, he chose to focus on what he called "exemplary people." He studied people such as Albert Einstein, Jane Addams, Eleanor Roosevelt, and Frederick Douglass rather than the mentally ill or neurotic. Instead of working with and diagnosing unhealthy behavior, he sought to understand what motivational factors drove healthy behavior. He focused on the top 1 percent of the population in his attempt to construct a model that would explain the forces that undergird individual performance. Maslow's theory was more fully expressed in his 1954 book *Motivation and Personality*.

Maslow's hierarchy is most often expressed in a pyramid, consisting of a five-tier model of human needs, with the most fundamental needs at the bottom and ascending ultimately to self-actualization at the top. The foundational layers of the pyramid contain what Maslow called "deficiency needs." These needs include basic physical needs, such as food, shelter, and clothing, followed by security. As these needs are met, love and belonging, along with self-esteem, become higher factors to be considered as one moves toward wholeness.

According to Maslow, the most basic level of needs must be met before an individual will strongly desire to pursue the secondary or higher-level needs. However, he also coined the term *metamotivation* to describe the motivation of people who go beyond the scope of basic needs and strive for constant betterment of themselves and others, often despite the fact that some of their own needs go unmet,[3]

In his early writings, self-actualization was the pinnacle of the pyramid. Self-actualization refers to the realization of one's full potential. Maslow described this level as the desire to accomplish everything one can, to become the most that one can be. But this description, while it speaks to personal growth, is all about the betterment of the individual and is centered on self and one's own fulfillment. While this concept was widely accepted, Maslow himself grew increasingly uncomfortable with the idea of a self-contained explanation of personal development and was challenged to consider that life is not complete until one rises above self alone and focuses on leaving a legacy of good for others. Through this challenge, he grew to believe that one must think beyond self if one is to truly impact the lives of others in a meaningful way.

In his later years, Maslow explored a further dimension of needs while criticizing his own vision on self-actualization. He came to realize that the self only finds its actualization in giving to some higher goal outside oneself, in altruism and spirituality, which is essentially the desire to reach the infinite. So, he added a new tier atop the pyramid called self-transcendence. Transcendence, for Maslow, referred to the very highest and most inclusive or holistic levels of human consciousness. It involved behaving and relating, as ends rather than means, to oneself and more especially to others. It meant being true to one's own values and seeking to improve the existence of others. Self-transcendence involved making a decision to become a value creator.[4]

It's interesting that Maslow eventually acknowledged that living in the highest order means living beyond self. That is not to suggest we should be unconcerned about having our basic needs met. If our deficiency needs are not met, it creates a dynamic that makes it very difficult for us to focus on ascending to higher levels of motivation. However, it's interesting to note that even Maslow acknowledged that many who were unable to have even their most basic physiological needs met could and often would ascend to the highest levels in service to others. This is exactly what he meant by metamotivation.

Self-transcendence means living beyond self. It's focusing on what we can do for others. It's creating a legacy of good. It's seeking to meet the needs of others and, in doing so, finding meaning and fulfillment in life personally. It's also counterintuitive: the secret to leading a meaningful and fulfilling life is actually found in generosity. The more we give, the more we will receive.

Generosity is living life with an open hand. Imagine trying to hold sand in the palm of your hand. If you were to make a fist to hold onto what you have, you would most certainly lose a good portion of it. And the tighter you squeeze, the more would escape between your fingers. But if you were to hold your hand open and cup your palm, your capacity would increase. When you have an open hand, others can take from you, but they can also add more as well. Living life with an open hand means living life with a greater capacity to both give and receive. The more you give, the more capacity you have to receive. If you surround yourself with value creators and you have a great capacity to receive, then you open yourself up to immense possibilities.

John Templeton is often quoted as having said, "To get joy, we must give it and to keep joy, we must scatter it." He is also often attributed with having said, "In order to be successful, focus on making others successful." Both are powerful statements that clearly express the heart of value creation.

> **Living life with an open hand means living life with a greater capacity to both give and receive.**

Surround yourself with value creators and as you give, it will be given to you. Not because you expect it. But by seeking to surround yourself with like-hearted individuals, you will also be surrounding yourself with people who have your best interest at heart. When you do that, a community of care and responsiveness prevails. This does not mean that those who receive from you will always be capable of reciprocating in kind. If that were the expectation, then it wouldn't be value creation. However, with each act of value creation, the recipient is charged with the responsibility to turn around and pay it forward. The purpose of value creation is to multiply acts of kindness in the world. The intent is to create movements of good and influence consumers toward being contributors. As George Bernard Shaw wrote in his play *Candida*, "We have no more right to consume happiness without producing it than to consume wealth without producing it."[5] Whether that charge is heeded, one may never know. But such a charge, nonetheless, should be inherent within each act of goodness.

Those who are value creators at heart and have been the recipients of value creation from others will hopefully multiply goodness, generating movements of good and enhancing the lives of others they encounter. So, if you find yourself in a situation in which your needs are constantly going unmet, then you may have to reevaluate the company you keep.

When a Situation Doesn't Improve

What if my situation doesn't improve? It's probably safe to assume that the folks who ask this question have found themselves in a situation in which value creation is being consistently met with value extraction. If enough unhealthy people are in the mix, then a value creator can feel like someone swimming in a muddy pond infested with leeches. Value extractors will attempt to attach themselves to value creators with the sole purpose of seeking to suck whatever life out of the creator they can.

This situation has caused many value creators to become discouraged and even begin to wonder if their actions were well founded. I want to offer words of both encouragement and caution. First, you never know the impact your actions may have on others. You may choose to give and never fully understand whether the actions you take will ever have a long-lasting positive impact. Give anyway—not because of the potential outcome but because giving is part and parcel of being a value creator.

It's also important to realize that one's giving may not have an immediate impact on the recipient. It may take time for them to fully feel the impact. This is especially true when the value creator is in relationship with someone who has been deeply hurt in the past or may be suffering from a serious lack of trust. That person may have erected self-protective defenses to prevent themselves from being hurt again. When a value creator senses this to be the case, compassion and patience are key. It may take time for the injured person to dismantle the protective emotional walls. Only a steady stream of value creation will ever erode these defenses and allow their true heart to emerge. Love them consistently.

At the same time, a word of caution is justified. If you find yourself in a situation in which you have given consistently and do not sense that the recipient is in a self-protective mode but rather is simply taking advantage of your gracious actions, then you may have to reevaluate the situation. You do not want to enable bad behavior. Do not think for a minute that servant leadership implies that there are no boundaries. Rather, setting boundaries may often be the only way a value extractor comes to terms with their destructive behavior.

Preventing Abuse

Whenever we sense that a value extractor is in the mix, we can follow a progression for addressing such individuals. Unless dealt with properly, value extractors will continue to suck the lifeblood out of those around them, damaging personal relationships and deterring collaborative endeavors. Value extractors must be addressed effectively. Let me suggest a three-step process for dealing with value extractors.

Step One: Carefrontation

Value extractors should initially be coached and encouraged to move beyond self. If their focus has been on self-promotion and self-protection, consuming rather than contributing, then they should be confronted with care. Left unaddressed, the behavior will continue, destroying inter-personal relationships and teams. Top-tier performance is based on trust and collaboration. Value extractors will short-circuit both. Like termites eating away at the integrity of a weight-bearing beam, they will find soft wood and begin to work their destructive ways until the decay is effectively addressed. Their negative impact may go undetected for a while, but sooner or later their corrosive power will weaken the relational constitution of any team.

When confronted with the self-serving nature of their actions, some may be horrified at the negative wake they have been creating. It may truly have been a blind spot that had never been exposed until that moment. If this is the case, then an air of humility and a commitment to change will reveal the individual's true heart. However, if they fail to heed the warning, then we must take corrective action. If the individual becomes defensive and casts aspersions on others, shifts blame and refuses to take responsibility, or resists engaging in deep personal introspection leading to change, then it's time to move on to step two.

Step Two: Isolation

Isolation provides an opportunity for self-reflection. It makes a clear statement about behavioral expectations and provides time for the person to make the necessary attitudinal adjustments. If their behavior persists, then the value extractor should be put in a "time-out" from the team. This may happen naturally as other team members simply fail to extend an invitation for that person to participate in projects. Or it may be necessary for the leader to quarantine the value extractor. The value extractor may be allowed to continue as an individual contributor for a season, but the team must be protected from their negative presence. In these cases, it's necessary to establish clear boundaries.

The individual must be told why such actions are being taken. It's a last resort in an attempt to help the individual to reflect on the negative impact their behavior is having on those around them. Ultimately, it's an attempt to restore the individual to full participation, but that depends entirely on the response of the one being isolated. If they can recognize the problem and commit to change, then they can be allowed to reengage with the team while being closely monitored to ensure they don't relapse. If the situation continues to deteriorate, then it may be necessary to excise the value extractor from the team and possibly the organization.

Step Three: Separation

Not everyone can be saved. You cannot help those who do not want to be helped. Some would prefer to destroy themselves and everyone around them rather than acknowledge their own need for growth. Some will simply slide down the Growth Spiral, resulting in alienation and desperation. When this happens, it's necessary to let them go. The quicker a leader can work through this progression with a value extractor, the better for the team. Whether the end result is restoration or release, it never does any good to postpone the inevitable. Givers need to set limits because takers rarely do.

Bold Leadership to Light the World

Value creation isn't for the timid. Because value creation is about putting others first, it demands that a person be totally committed to being a giver. It requires sacrifice. It means being consciously aware of the impact that one is making in the lives of others. Being a value creation–focused leader isn't for the faint of heart either. Such leaders must lead by example. Additionally, they must coach and encourage their team members to play well in the sandbox together. And when the team members don't, bold leadership is required to confront and address value extraction for the destructive force that it is.

Conversely, when value creation is woven into the fabric of a team, productivity is compounded. Trust is elevated. Collaboration becomes the norm and innovation is the by-product as people begin to work together to solve existing problems. When values are clear and everyone is aligned, valucentricity creates a circuit through which energy can flow to light up the world and spawn movements of good. High morale and goodwill begin to permeate the organization, escalating performance. Customers, both internally and externally, are impacted in positive ways that enhance respect and engender loyalty. Good things happen and the world becomes a better place.

Some may consider value creation to be on the softer side of leadership because of its interpersonal overtones. But the reality is that building a sense of community demands vigilance that only the fiercest proponents of culture may master. If you want to make the work world a brighter place through value creation, then you must pursue it with boldness that commands awe and respect.

Recently a new species of deep-water shark was discovered near the Northwestern Hawaiian Islands. Measurements, along with specific external markings and patterns, confirmed that it was a new species in the lanternshark family—the *Etmopterus lailae*. Lanternsharks are actually one of the most species-rich shark genera, with approximately thirty-eight known species. Eleven of these species have been discovered since 2002.

Lanternsharks are one of two shark families to be bioluminescent. In other words, they are glow-in-the-dark sharks. Bioluminescence is the emission of light as a result of a biochemical reaction. In contrast to fluorescence and phosphorescence, bioluminescent reactions do not require the initial absorption of sunlight or other electromagnetic radiation by a molecule or pigment in order to emit light. It happens purely as an internal reaction without external stimulation. It's within its own constitution to shine. Though small, these sharks can put off quite a glow. *Etmopterus lailae* is a tiny yet tenacious and luminous shark.[6]

I am fascinated by the idea of a glow-in-the-dark shark. Sharks inspire awe and respect. They are the masters of their domain. No matter their size, they move with confidence, grace, and power. Pound for pound, they are tough characters. But sharks are typically predators that prefer to maintain a low profile. That way they can sneak up on their prey without alerting them to the danger of their presence. Sharks that light up are novel and defy reason.

For some, the idea of being a value creator defies reason or comes across as weakness. Because value creators see the benefit of collaboration over competition, some believe such an attitude produces vulnerabilities in corporate ecosystems that call for the survival of the fittest. Nothing could be further from the truth. Value creation requires a leader to be bold enough to fight through the fears associated with such a philosophy. It requires strong leadership to confront value extractors before they can do damage to teams. Value creators are tough and tenacious in maintaining a strong sense of values and personal conviction. They are both transparent and luminescent. No matter their role, title, or position, they have a massive influence on their environment. They create a sense of awe and respect throughout the pools in which they swim. And they are to be feared by value extractors because they will not allow anyone to compromise valucentricity. In short, value creators can be sharks and glow in the dark too. So, be bold in your leadership and light it up!

›› GAINING TRACTION: Questions for Consideration & Application

1. What fears impede a leader's ability to lead?

2. How could you effectively address each one of those fears?

3. Why is self-transcendence so much more powerful than self-actualization?

4. What is the best way to deal with a value extractor?

5. What are some ways you could more effectively "glow in the dark" as a leader?

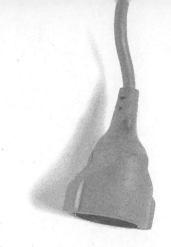

BUILD BOLD RELATIONSHIPS:
ACCOUNTABILITY

NINE

ROW, ROW, ROW YOUR BOAT

Character—the willingness to accept responsibility for one's own life—is the source from which self-respect springs.

—Joan Didion

My family and I have frequently enjoyed taking rafting trips down the Ocoee and the Chattooga rivers in Tennessee and South Carolina. Both provide wild and scenic rides down stretches of challenging rapids as well as respites of recreational rafting. Those who brave the currents witness spectacular rock formations and a wide variety of flora and fauna. I have often leveraged these adventures to casually teach my kids about teamwork. Much can be learned while rafting on the river, as long as you keep your paddle in the water and your rear in the raft. If you don't, then there are a lot of lessons to be learned about survival.

Maybe you remember the following children's nursery rhyme lyrics you sang during childhood:

> *Row, row, row your boat*
> *Gently down the stream.*
> *Merrily, merrily, merrily, merrily,*
> *Life is but a dream.*

It's a memorable little ditty, filled with powerful life lessons in the chorus alone, that sticks with you for a lifetime. It's by no means an exhaustive taxonomy on leadership. Nonetheless, contained within its short rhyme are some profound insights that serve as reminders of basic principles that can guide leaders in evoking strong individual and team performance. Let me expound.

Row, Row, Row

For teams to be effective, everyone must row. Not only must everyone row, but they must row, row, row. And they must row in cadence with one another. Rowing can be fun, but it is frequently hard. Those who row must work together to create momentum. In addition to propelling your craft, rowing also aids in setting the course. Pulling together is the only way to navigate the river while avoiding the hazards. When it comes to teams, there can be no slackers. Each person must do their part if the whole is going to be successful. And, they must row in a coordinated fashion. If one person chooses not to row with the rest, it can be disastrous. When rowers are synchronized, they can be extremely efficient and effective in maneuvering the vessel down the river while maximizing each stroke.

If their cadence is off, or someone willfully chooses to stroke independently, it can quickly put everyone in a precarious situation. Not only must everyone row, but they must also have a rhythm to their rowing. If their cadence does not coordinate with their effort, then they waste energy and confusion abounds. The leader, through clear communication, must establish the rowers' rhythm. In sculling, the person responsible for setting the cadence is the coxswain. In a raft, the guide typically mans the helm at the aft and calls the commands to provide safety, speed, and direction. Both must communicate clearly to all onboard if they are to navigate the river or race successfully. The same holds true of a team leader. Roles and responsibilities must be designated clearly before the adventure begins. And the role of the leader is to coordinate everyone's efforts.

Instructions must be given and expectations clarified before an oar or paddle touches the water. Once the team is on the water, signals must be clear and concise. Without clarity in the cadence, teams flounder. Without clear vision, people can perish. It's the responsibility of the leader to guide and protect all who are on the vessel by giving clear direction and providing the cadence that allows everyone to pull together. The responsibility of the leader is to give direction and provide protection.

Clarity and unity are both necessary for there to be productivity. If either is missing, then teams will flounder for lack of momentum and direction.

Your Boat

While this may sound a bit elemental, the reality is that you can and only should seek to *row your own boat*. You cannot row someone else's boat for them. It is a huge mistake for someone to assume responsibility or make excuses for someone else who is acting irresponsibly. While we have talked about the need for leaders to provide strong coaching and developmental opportunities for their team members, some people simply will not row and you cannot will them to row if they do not want to. Simply put, you cannot help people who do not want help. And some people just do not want help. They are either unwilling to receive it or refuse to assume personal responsibility for making the personal change necessary to be a productive team member.

This is where boundaries come into play. You can instruct. You can seek to inspire. You can provide resources for personal and professional development. But at some point, every person must make their own decision as to how they intend to row their own boat. Leaders cannot and must not assume responsibility for team members who refuse to row. To do so enables bad behavior. If their role is to man a solo craft, then they must assume responsibility for the pace and direction of their own boat. If they are part of a team, then they must be held accountable to row in a synchronized fashion with others. Not to do so can jeopardize the success of the journey.

If a person refuses to put their oar in the water, then it's the leader's role to address the situation and hold that person accountable. At some point, a good leader must have the sense to say, "Hey, that's not my boat." At times, it's necessary to cut someone loose and let them drift if they have tied their boat to yours or their presence is impeding progress. As Peter Drucker has said, "Executives owe it to the organization and their fellow workers not to tolerate nonperforming people."[1]

Good leaders seek to inspire elevated performance. They encourage, reward, and recognize positive movement. They provide resources for personal and professional growth. They create environments conducive for collaboration and

> **Leaders cannot and must not assume responsibility for team members who refuse to row.**

innovation. And, when necessary, they make hard calls to provide security and protect the integrity of their teams. They do this by ensuring that everyone rows and that they row their own boat effectively.

Gently Down the Stream

It is always easier to row when you are floating downstream. But the reality is that you rarely drift to a desired destination. Occasionally you do experience long stretches of lazy river that allow you to kick back and relax, enjoying the sun and scenery. During these times, you can rest and recuperate while planning for the big water that you know lies just around the next bend. But on the river, and in the marketplace, oftentimes everyone is called on to muster their full energy to paddle against the current and maneuver the vessel to avoid harm or reach a particular destination. These are the times when the team is tested, when the true nature of the team is revealed. Tough times reveal what good times conceal. The challenges of the adventure will show clearly who possesses grit and determination.

Difficult times will also expose those who prefer to paddle only in a downstream direction.

Merrily, Merrily, Merrily, Merrily

It's no secret that happy people are more productive. The challenge lies in the fact that it's extremely difficult to make unhappy people happy. But leaders try to do it all the time. They think that by giving certain people perks and privileges they are somehow going to be able to turn a sour person into a soaring performer.

This rarely happens. People who are unhappy by nature are very difficult to reform. Rather than try to turn a frog into a prince, why not just hire princes? Quit wishing and hoping while you are kissing frogs. Start doing a better job of selecting new team members whose values, beliefs, and behaviors mirror those you want reflected in the organization. Then, and only then, will you be able to build stellar teams of people who enjoy rowing together.

Happy teams have high engagement. Happy teams collaborate, innovate, and celebrate together. Happy teams believe the best in one another, want the best for one another, and expect the best from one another. Happy teams engender loyalty, experience higher morale, and garner discretionary effort. Happy teams produce!

Life Is but a Dream

In an attempt to provide good coaching and consultation to executives, I used to ask them, "What concerns keep you awake at night?" I thought that if we could resolve the issues that caused them to lose sleep, then we were offering a valuable service. It was not altogether a bad approach. However, over time I began to realize there was a far more powerful question that could navigate us into better water. So, I switched my leading question.

Now, the first question I typically ask a leader is, "What are you so passionate about that it causes you to spring out of bed in the morning?" Their answer becomes their North Star. It gives direction and guidance to all subsequent conversations.

The North Star, also known as Polaris, is the most important star in the sky. Because it's the most important, many might think it's also the brightest. But it isn't. In fact, it pales in comparison to many other stars, coming in at forty-eighth in terms of brightness. Polaris is so important because Earth's axis points almost directly at it. This means that during the course of the night, Polaris remains in virtually the same spot above the northern horizon year-round while the other stars circle around it. It neither rises nor sets, providing a constant point of reference by which to navigate. It can always be found in a due northerly direction. Likewise, an individual's passion serves as their personal Polaris, giving direction to all their decision-making. Passion is the pivotal point around which all other considerations revolve.

> **An individual's passion serves as their personal Polaris, giving direction to all their decision-making.**

If you are wondering how this relates to leadership, it's quite simple. Passion always shows someone's priorities (what one values). And one's priorities are the surefire path to productivity. If you want to help people shine their brightest, then try fanning the flame within them rather than constantly trying to light a fire under them. The greatest act of leadership is to help people connect their personal passion to corporate objectives. When you do that, you produce passionate performance. Excitement will mount when people are encouraged to leverage their passion and strengths to solve problems. That is when people begin to spring out of bed in the morning, energized by what they do. And that is when leaders can sleep soundly through the night because they have drafted and crafted dream teams. When you lead dream teams, life becomes a dream.

> **The greatest act of leadership is to help people connect their personal passion to corporate objectives.**

Make Sure Everyone's OAR Is in the Water

When it comes to building dream teams, one of the most critical concerns is making sure everyone's OAR is in the water. By OAR, I am referring to elements that must be present for team members to bring their best effort to each endeavor. OAR is an acrostic, which stands for ownership, accountability, and responsibility. These three essential elements ensure that the third prong of a remarkable culture—*expecting the best from one another*—becomes a reality. When these three elements are present, leaders spend less time micromanaging people and more time releasing and resourcing them to reach extraordinary levels of customer service both internally and externally. Let's talk about why all three of these elements are necessary to produce elevated performance.

Ownership

Ownership empowers people to take responsibility for creating value. An owner has a far greater vested interest in the outcome of any endeavor than someone who has merely been tasked with the responsibility of managing it. When someone feels as if they own the process, they become much more emotionally attached to the results.

We have two teenage boys still at home, and our house tends to be the hangout of choice for their friends, which we love. The only downside is that our fridge and pantry are constantly raided, necessitating frequent runs to the store to replenish supplies. Because of our heavy travel schedules, my wife and I share household responsibilities. When I do the grocery shopping, I try to time my trip to our local market to coincide with when I know Wanda is working her checkout counter.

Let me describe Wanda. She is a delightful woman in her midsixties, with a thick mane of greying hair that she usually braids and a smile that could light up Times Square. She is one of the happiest people I know, and she makes shopping a pleasure. Her checkout lane is always busy with customers, but no one seems to mind waiting a little longer to linger in her presence because she has an uncanny way of making your day just a little bit better. She knows many of her customers by name and is familiar with their family members, having met them on previous visits. She engages each person in meaningful conversation and truly expresses interest and concern about not only their shopping experience but also them personally. She is quick to reach into her drawer and pull out coupons so each patron can save a few bucks. More importantly, she has this ability to reach into a person's heart, providing just the right word of encouragement to bring a smile to their face. She knows how to connect with others. And she does so with one purpose—to brighten their day.

I once caught Wanda when she was on a break and asked her about the source of her extraordinary customer service. Her reply was nothing short of remarkable. She looked me straight in the eyes and said, "Life can be tough. But when people come into my lane, I want them to forget, for just a moment, all their concerns and to feel cared for. My mission is to put a smile on their face. If I can do that, I've done something good—and that makes me feel good."

Wanda "owns" twelve feet of counter space at our local grocery store. It's one of thousands of supermarkets across the country that bear the same name. She does not own the store. She does not own the cash register, or even the candies and periodicals that adorn the counter. But she owns the relationship with every single customer she encounters. When they come through her lane, she owns their experience. She is on a mission to make their day. And she does it with unswerving devotion. As a result, her managers leave her alone to do her thing. They sit back and marvel at how she earns the loyalty of customers. If they could bottle her enthusiasm, they would. But what she does cannot be multiplied through process. Process can never replicate passion. Process may ensure quality and consistency, but passion is personal.

When individuals are allowed to assume ownership of their work, it becomes personal. They are free to bring the best of who they are to the endeavor. If they are given the freedom to be creative, they can develop deep emotional attachment to their work by putting their own fingerprints all over the process. Rather than working by rote, they can make it relationally rich. And when it becomes relationally rich, it also becomes emotionally rewarding. Value is created and problems are solved as they take more personal pride in the fact that the work is a reflection of them. Work becomes a form of personal expression. How we work shows who we truly are. Healthy people want to grow and make a meaningful contribution to a worthy endeavor. They want to make a positive wake in the world. The key to good leadership begins by empowering people to take ownership of the process.

> **When individuals are allowed to assume ownership of their work, it becomes personal. They are free to bring the best of who they are to the endeavor.**

Accountability

If you want people to take ownership of the process and be responsible for the results, then you have to empower them with the authority to make the decisions necessary to make it happen. To give responsibility without authority will lead to frustration. If the individual entrusted with a task or project has to continually come back for permission to pull the trigger, then you haven't delegated with authority. Authority simply means the person is acting with full authorization to move forward as they deem best. With authority comes accountability.

To be accountable for something means that a person is obliged to report, explain, or justify their actions. They are answerable for the results their actions produce. Accountability in some circles has gotten a bad rap. For some it implies micromanagement or heavy supervisory oversight. Neither need be the case. *Accountability* is not a dirty word. It simply means you are willing to submit yourself to checks and balances and the reporting necessary to keep any endeavor on course. It means you are willing to play ball in such a way as to not fumble your responsibilities.

> *Accountability* **is not a dirty word. It means you are willing to play ball in such a way as to not fumble your responsibilities.**

When everyone is held accountable, details are thoroughly covered and deadlines are met because actions are coordinated. Gaps are closed. Information flows freely and collaboration is encouraged to maximize the talent of the team. Accountability breeds awareness. And awareness creates synergy because each person knows what others are doing and is able to leverage their strengths effectively.

Many have endured the mind-numbing corporate torture of death by meetings. Poorly conducted meetings are not only a waste of time, they are an atrocity. A general team meeting serves only three purposes. The first is to clarify strategic direction. Where do we want to go? What is the big picture? Tactics, objectives, and initiatives all flow from strategy. These tactics, objectives, and initiatives can be handled either individually or in huddles of subgroups. Do not bore everyone and bog down the process by enumerating details that only a few team members need to know.

The second purpose of a meeting is to assign responsibilities. Who is going to be in charge of making sure any given base is covered? Roles need to be clarified so that there are lines of demarcation regarding the work. Thirdly, a general meeting should be used to enhance accountability. This provides each person or team an opportunity to give an update on the progress they are making. The updates do not need to be exhaustive. This is simply an opportunity to provide assurance that those elements of the project that are under each team's purview are being responsibly addressed.

Accountability keeps everyone on course and encourages the communication necessary to coordinate efforts. This efficiency helps everyone accomplish tasks in a timely manner. It also intercepts entropy at its earliest stages so as to avoid wasting energy.

Accountability flows from a sense of ownership. When people own the process, they are accountable for the results.

Responsibility

Ownership and accountability require people to act responsibly to get the work done. When someone is responsible, they are entrusted with the power to control or manage the process. Because they are accountable for the results, they seek the resources necessary to make whatever they are entrusted to do happen.

Acting responsibly is a sign of maturity. When someone acts responsibly, it means they can be counted on to accomplish the task. When everyone acts responsibly, all the bases are covered and much can be accomplished. However, if one person does not do their work or does not do it well, then that person's irresponsibility becomes someone else's responsibility. When team members are forced to carry the load meant for others, morale tends to wane. Of course, there will always be times when the team is called to rally during a crisis or an approaching deadline. However, if an additional ask becomes commonplace, then the burden may quickly become unbearable.

One of the first signs of poor leadership is taxing good team members with picking up the slack for someone else's poor performance rather than holding the individual responsible accountable to do the work and do it well. When this becomes the pattern, good people tend to leave the organization in droves. While it may be easier to ask someone else to make up the deficit, this shortsighted solution can lead to long-term negative consequences. If people do not act responsibly and are not willing to be held accountable to take ownership of the process and produce stellar results, then strong developmental conversations are required to maintain team integrity. If these conversations do not move the needle toward mature and responsible activity, then leadership needs to make changes in personnel.

Though the *Row, Row, Row Your Boat* chorus is familiar to many, most do not recall the last stanza. The last few lines are actually a bit of an oddity. After having expounded upon some of the many benefits of rowing and the virtues of those who do, the last verse concludes the childhood ditty with a conundrum. It says:

> *Row, row, row your boat,*
> *Gently down the stream.*
> *Ha-ha, fooled you all.*
> *I'm a submarine.*

Occasionally, while trying to get teams to row together, you may discover that not everyone is on board. You may come to the realization that someone isn't in the boat at all. If they have fallen overboard and are in peril, then do everything within your power to save them. But if they never got on your boat and you discover they're actually in a submarine, that's another situation altogether. If that is the case, by all means, do not allow them to torpedo your efforts. As a leader intent on preserving the safety and protecting the integrity of your team, you may be forced to take evasive action. And, if necessary, go to DEFCON and eliminate the threat before you see a bubble trail in the water.

>> **GAINING TRACTION: Questions for Consideration & Application**

1. It has been said that "tough times reveal what good times conceal." Give some examples or observations from your personal experience that confirm this statement.

2. What is the difference between ownership, accountability, and responsibility? Why is each essential to delegation?

3. What are the three purposes of a team meeting?

4. How could you restructure your team meetings to be more effective?

5. What were your greatest takeaways from this chapter?

TEN

RULES OF ENGAGEMENT

Words, so innocent and powerless as they are, as standing in a dictionary, how potent for good and evil they become in the hands of one who knows how to combine them.

—Nathaniel Hawthorne

The term *rules of engagement* (ROE) commonly refers to military directives meant to describe the circumstances under which forces will enter into and continue to engage in conflict with other existing forces. They are the orders issued by a competent military authority that delineate when, where, how, and against whom military force may be used. Rules of engagement are the result of a general recognition that procedures and standards are essential in formulating appropriate conduct and effectiveness in civilized warfare. Historically, this notion that civilized warfare must be regulated has been backed by a long list of international treaties and agreements. The most significant of these treaties is the Geneva Convention, which outlines the treatment of prisoners of war and civilians.[1]

During the Cold War, both the Soviet Union and the United States came to the realization that the potential advantages of attacking were not worth the consequences of retaliation. To prevent a minor incident from provoking nuclear warfare, they were inspired to establish procedures defining allowable actions. Without these rules of engagement, circumstances of conflict could easily spiral out of control and result in the decimation of masses.

Wherever people gather, there will inevitably be offense and conflict. We are, after all, human. This, of course, includes the work environment. If leaders want to preserve a healthy corporate culture and build strong teams, they must recognize this reality and find a clear path through which conflict may be resolved. Failure to proactively provide a plan for conflict resolution is to ensure implosion. And the best way to preempt bad behavior in the sandbox is to establish rules of engagement for teams.

> **Failure to proactively provide a plan for conflict resolution is to ensure implosion.**

No Throwing Sand

When I was in preschool, my favorite time of day was when we would go outside to the playground after lunch. It gave me the opportunity to burn off the excess energy that had been building for hours in a claustrophobic classroom. On the playground were swings, slides, monkey bars, and my favorite of all—the sandbox, where kid commandos could set up miniature military figures and play war.

One of our first skirmishes was so memorable that it left an impression on me that lingers to this day. Charlie and Robert had drawn a line in the sand and thrown down the gauntlet, challenging Mitch and me to rally our forces. They proceeded to build a makeshift bunker with a plastic sand shovel and established a stronghold to serve as their command center. Mitch and I created a fortified wall with some sticks we had gathered from under a big oak tree. When our miniature fighting forces were in position, we took turns lobbing a baseball into the war zone from opposite ends of the sandbox. Whichever figures came into contact with the baseball were eliminated from the battlefield. The army left with the last man standing was declared the victor.

Charlie initiated the aerial assault with the well-scuffed white orb. It dealt a deadly blow, wiping out a significant number of our shooters and two flamethrowers as it crashed through our line of defense. Our subsequent attack was equally effective and we alternated back and forth until only a handful of characters remained on the dunes of the contained desert. When it was his turn, Robert launched a precision strike. It was a thing of beauty. With a slight backspin and high arc, the stitched cannonball landed on the backside of a dune and careened at a perfect angle, sliding in the direction of our last four action figures. We all leaned in to ascertain the effect of the aerial assault. Then, with dramatic flare incited by mild frustration, Mitch used both of his hands to scoop a mound of sand and launch it into the air to emulate a vast explosion. Before any of us could duck for cover, the damage was done. A cloud of sand shrapnel temporarily blinded Charlie, Robert, and me. We spent the better part of the afternoon dusting the granular debris out of our hair and clothing. We had all learned a valuable lesson.

Before we took arms on the battlefield the following day, we had established a single rule of engagement: *Under no circumstances was anyone to throw sand!*

More than fifty years later, I still remember that afternoon on the playground. And to this day, I still seek to help teams apply that single commitment as I coach and lead them to pursue healthier relationships in the workplace.

Relational Rules of Engagement

If you have to have a single rule of engagement, *No Throwing Sand* is a pretty good one. As we have said, conflict is inevitable. It's the ability or inability to resolve conflict that will either enhance or diminish the effectiveness of teams. Resolving conflict effectively necessitates rules of engagement, setting forth principles and expectations as to how team members will treat one another. The purpose of such rules is to maintain a spirit of unity. That is not to suggest that everyone will share the same opinion but rather that everyone will have a common commitment to practice healthy forms of interpersonal communication when stressful situations, disagreements, and offenses arise.

These rules of engagement do not have to be exhaustive. Human resource departments are notorious for creating voluminous policies and procedures manuals to cover a broad array of interpersonal contingencies. The challenge is that once you have created a massive handbook of regulations, you have to enforce them by establishing a sort of police state to monitor and manage those who most likely never read the manual in the first place. I would like to suggest a much simpler solution. Give a few guidelines and expect people to act like adults. If they don't, then coach them. After coaching, if they continue to throw sand, then you may have to restrict them from playing with everyone else at recess.

For the sake of simplicity, let me offer up five suggestions that, when applied consistently, could resolve the vast majority of workplace conflicts. We will call them relational rules of engagement. Each is stated with a first-person pronoun, reflecting what must be a personal commitment on the part of each team member.

1. I will talk to you before I ever talk about you.

Conflict is frequently exacerbated by gossip. Watercooler conversation cannot resolve issues with those who are not present. It simply taints the relational pool by spreading negativity to others who likely have nothing to do with the conflict and can play little role in its resolution. Side conversations and gossip can poison the atmosphere more than mustard gas.

People frequently engage in these conversations in an attempt to gain support for their position or justify their reaction to what they may deem to be unfair treatment. Like children playing Red Rover, they seek anyone who will come over to their side to garner the emotional support they desire. But when others are involved unnecessarily in a personal offense, the circle of conflict expands and collateral damage increases. Once other people have been asked to pick up an

177

offense, it becomes far more difficult to go back and clear the air with those who are now carrying a negative impression based on hearsay.

When someone speaks about an individual who isn't present, the story can easily be misrepresented to bolster the position of the person who is speaking. The person who is being called into question cannot explain or defend their position, so it isn't possible to draw an unbiased conclusion. Like a spider spinning a web to entangle its prey, the one who gossips is seeking to emotionally entangle others in a relationally deadly game.

Casting aspersions on someone is akin to throwing sand in the air in an attempt to blind those nearby from being able to see the situation through objective eyes. As my buddies and I agreed on the playground, under no circumstances is anyone to throw sand.

The mature way to handle conflict is for the person who has been offended to go directly to the offender and attempt to work through the issues in private. If both individuals can conduct themselves with a spirit of openness and humility, then a quick resolution is often possible.

2. I will engage in candid conversations with humility, knowing I have room to grow.

Whether we are confronting someone or the one being confronted, it requires humility to be able to fully engage in a sensitive conversation without getting defensive or overly emotional. When emotion escalates, so does defensiveness. And becoming defensive is counterproductive. Once we become defensive, we are in essence saying we have no room to grow. We become more intent on justifying our position than we are on exploring and learning. Emotion can run deep, but when it hijacks the conversation, it's rarely productive. It could be said that as emotions rise, intelligence falls. Often in the heat of emotion, we say stupid stuff and take dumb and destructive actions.

The key to remaining calm and not becoming defensive is to readily admit that we have much to learn. If we can remain curious rather than callous, then we can seek to understand the perspective of the other person and not merely defend our own. If we view one another as advisors rather than adversaries, then we can seek to extract insights from the conversation that may enhance our emotional intelligence. Our sensitivities can be sharpened and our communication skills honed when we are open to hear how our words and actions have impacted others.

Remember, healthy people want to grow. And relationship catalyzes growth. When someone cares enough about the relationship to come to you directly, you should honor that they are attempting to make things right with you in the correct way rather than talking behind your back.

Keep the focus on what you need to learn. It's easy to focus on what you think the other person needs to know. This causes many to slip into a tit-for-tat kind of conversation in an attempt to balance the scales. Conversation that degenerates to this level immediately becomes scorekeeping

> **If we can remain curious rather than callous, then we can seek to understand the perspective of the other person and not merely defend our own.**

and quickly loses its impact. It very well may be that the people to whom you are speaking need to examine their perspective and approach, but save that for a subsequent developmental conversation.

The key here is to enter into the conversation with humility and openness, seeking to learn what you can to connect more deeply with the other person. If that person reciprocates in seeking your feedback in order to learn, then you may have the opportunity to offer feedback for growth. If not, then work through the issues at hand and come back at another time if you feel it necessary to explore further issues related to the other person's growth and development.

3. We will seek objective input if we come to an impasse.

We would be naïve to think that all conflict could be resolved simply by engaging in direct conversation with someone else. Defensiveness, blind spots, and triggers can easily impede our ability to effectively address issues that come between us and another person. Conversations can quickly slide sideways. Emotions can run amuck. Sparks can fly, despite our best intentions. And we can sometimes find ourselves spinning our wheels in an attempt to get the other person to see the situation from our perspective. If we find ourselves in a stalemate, we may need to seek objective outside input in order to get things off dead center and hopefully on track.

This is where the insight of a coach, mentor, counselor, or human resource specialist can play a significant role in resolving the conflict. An objective outsider—someone who has no vested interest other than the growth of both parties—can serve to clarify the issues and help move the conversation toward reconciliation. Every organization should have someone whom it trusts, either internally or externally, who can provide guidance in conflict resolution.

Conflict will inevitably arise. We must have a clear commitment to take our issues and grievances directly to the person or parties involved. We must be committed to reconciling and pursuing unity. But all of this does not guarantee that both parties will have the emotional intelligence or maturity to navigate rough relational waters effectively. Organizations that place an emphasis on culture will ensure that coaching resources are available for those who need assistance to navigate interpersonal conflict with objectivity and clarity.

4. I recognize that the objective of the conversation is to seek understanding, resolve issues, and move toward unity.

It's important to state once again that even the best organizations and teams are not conflict-free. However, strong culture requires a clear commitment to the quick resolution of conflicts and the protection of relational integrity. Unity should never be misconstrued as like-mindedness. Diversity of thought is absolutely necessary to promote growth and innovation. However, like-heartedness, the commitment to certain organizational values, and the willingness to work through issues to seek deeper understanding is critical if we want to pursue relational health.

Unity means we have come to a deeper understanding of one another and that understanding has allowed us to connect on a more personal level. While we may not always agree, we have a commitment to help one another grow. That growth will hopefully lead to a greater sense of personal enlightenment that will allow us to move toward maturity, expanding our capability to relate more effectively to one another. This amounts to having one another's best interest at heart. It may ultimately lead to the acknowledgment of our differences. But, more importantly, it should lead to an affirmation of our common values on which we can build a better future relationally.

This is not a matter of conflict management but rather conflict resolution. We must be committed to staying in the tunnel of chaos until we see the light. We must demonstrate the emotional fortitude to stick it out in constructive conversations until we feel we have reached a new level of understanding and respect for one another. And, at the very least, we acknowledge that we can disagree without dishonoring or disrespecting one another. We will remain steadfast in our commitment to relational integrity.

5. I will forgive quickly.

When a matter has been settled and the issues resolved, move on. Ruminating on relational failure can be demoralizing. Those involved should mark the lessons learned and make a commitment to grow beyond the limitations exposed through the conversation. Frequently revisiting the offenses can be life-draining. Holding grudges garners nothing good.

Unresolved offenses can certainly become rancorous. It's equally toxic to work through difficulties only to have them revisited during subsequent tension-filled encounters. Forgiveness is the conscious commitment to move beyond the problem and not hold the issue over someone's head. Forgiveness is the act of pardoning or no longer holding someone responsible for making things right. It means remitting or canceling a debt or obligation. Forgiveness means the issue has been resolved in one's spirit. The future is unfettered by past actions when forgiveness is offered. Forgiveness is emotionally disentangling oneself from the anger and frustration brought about by the actions of another.

When an individual is unable to forgive, dregs of doubt remain. These suspicions may continue to taint the relationship, making someone prone to looking for signs that the issue still remains. These suspicions can morph into self-fulfilling prophecies, as the one jaded by an inability to forgive may interpret certain actions in light of their suspicions. They literally begin to see what they are looking for and the problem is compounded. The emotional baggage continues to pile up.

> **The future is unfettered by past actions when forgiveness is offered.**

If the problem arises again, then it should be addressed without the emotional distress that may have been created by the previous encounter. Boundaries may need to be established to curtail bad behavior. The idea is to intercept the entropy before it becomes a problematic pattern. Sometimes it's necessary to address an issue on multiple occasions before the perpetrator clearly sees the destructive nature of their activity. How many times someone is willing to address an issue depends on several factors. These factors may include:

1. The severity of the action.
2. The potential negative consequences if the behavior continues.
3. The depth of the relationship.
4. Whether humility is present.
5. A solid commitment to change, including seeking the resources necessary to realize the desired change.

If there is a commitment to continue the relationship, then forgiveness wipes the emotional slate clean and allows both parties to move into the future without being constrained by the failures of the past. True forgiveness frees the offender from the fear that past failures will be resurrected as artillery to be used against them in future encounters. More importantly, forgiveness frees the offended from the burden of being bogged down in a morass of mind-numbing negativity. Forgiveness gives each party the freedom to leave failure in the past and focus on building a brighter future. Forgiveness is the art of finding balance between downloading emotionally harmful debris, while establishing healthy boundaries so that bad behavior is curtailed.

Relational rules of engagement are guidelines that govern conflict resolution. They are a general recognition that certain expectations are essential in formulating appropriate conduct as to how we should relate to one another under duress. When we are committed to dealing with one another directly and respectfully, culture is enhanced. The strongest organizations are not conflict-free but rather have a commitment to maintaining unity by working through conflict to resolution.

›› GAINING TRACTION: Questions for Consideration & Application

1. How would it impact relationships in your organization if everyone made a simple commitment to "talk to others directly to resolve issues rather than talking about them"?

2. In what ways can you remain curious when you are dealing with conflict resolution?

3. What resources are available for assistance when people reach an impasse in pursuing conflict resolution?

4. When we say unity is the goal of conflict resolution, what does that look like? What does it not look like?

5. Why is forgiveness such an important part of conflict resolution?

6. What role do boundaries play in conflict resolution?

ELEVEN

RAW CONVERSATIONS

As human beings, our job in life is to help people realize how rare and valuable each one of us really is, that each of us has something that no one else has—or ever will have—something inside that is unique to all time. It's our job to encourage each other to discover that uniqueness and to provide ways of developing its expression.

—Fred Rogers

Performance appraisals have become standard business practice. Performance management systems are employed to manage and align an organization's resources to achieve its highest possible performance. These evaluations have historically been conducted annually, but many organizations are now moving toward more frequent review cycles. A growing body of evidence suggests that the more frequent the feedback, the more "on task" individuals and teams tend to be.

In my experience, highly performing teams receive the benefit of continual coaching. The more frequently the leader can provide insightful feedback, aligning personal passion and organizational objectives, the more productive individuals and teams will be. This means leaders must make it a priority to be engaged in open, candid, and continual conversations with those whom they lead. Frequently, these conversations need to be RAW.

The term *RAW* refers to frank and candid conversation. RAW is an acrostic that incorporates the three components of this type of developmental conversation: reality, advancement, and wrestling. It may sometimes be painful, but it's real, authentic, and to the heart. Providing RAW feedback is to pursue authenticity one conversation at a time. Strong cultures are crafted by providing continual feedback and making necessary adjustments. RAW conversations put issues and suspicions out on the table so they may be adequately addressed, allowing for transparency and hopefully reinforcing trust. Organizations that employ RAW conversations effectively create environments conducive to employees believing the best in one another.

RAW conversations are developmental conversations designed to provide encouragement, coaching, and correction. According to Gallup, few workers believe their managers lead in an inspirational way by developing them and helping them grow. Yet Gallup estimates that managers account for at least 70 percent of variance in employee engagement across business units.[1] Part of the reason for this could be directly attributed to the fact that many leaders are intimidated by the prospect of confronting those who are poorly performing and offering the resources necessary for them to improve. There is an obvious need for leaders to sharpen their skill sets when it comes to offering clear and constructive feedback.

The Purpose of RAW Conversations

RAW conversations are conducted for personal developmental purposes and relational centering. They are to be conducted one-on-one, precipitated when an individual is in need of correction, coaching, mentoring, or encouragement. These conversations are not limited to a leader and a direct report. They may be between colleagues and peers or can even be used to "coach up" throughout the organization. The purpose of a RAW conversation is threefold and is captured in the acrostic of the name itself.

1. *Reveal reality.*

  Leadership at its best deals in reality. Good leaders do not spin, hedge, or distort reality. Reality is not what you may think or want to think it is. Reality is not what you hope or would prefer to believe it to be. It is not what you wish or pray it should be. But reality is seeing any situation for what it actually is.

  Edwin Friedman states it best when he writes, "In any situation, the person who can most accurately describe reality without laying blame will emerge as the leader, whether designated or not." Essentially, what Friedman is saying is that those with good leadership skills call it like it is. Good leadership does not avoid addressing the elephant in the room or deflect from the issue at hand by attempting to create an alternate reality.

In the south, we are fond of saying, "Whatever is down in your well will eventually come up in your bucket." It's just another way of saying that reality always shows up. It's just a matter of time. And when it does, the person who has most accurately described it will emerge the leader.

Sometimes leaders are afraid to call it as they see it. They may be fearful that their perspective is skewed. They may be fearful of offending someone. They may be engaged in corporate politics or attempting to remain politically correct. Whatever the reason, few leaders have the intestinal fortitude to simply speak the truth. The consequences of being disingenuous or too cowardly to address reality are too numerous to set forth at this time. Suffice it to say that reality will ultimately rule. Therefore, it's in everyone's best interest to identify and deal with reality effectively. Good leaders are ruthless about dealing in reality.

RAW conversations, when conducted appropriately, accurately describe reality. In doing so, they serve as beacons of light to illuminate the path of personal development and team productivity.

2. *Advance creative dialogue.*

The second purpose of RAW conversations is to advance the conversation by exploring creative options. These conversations serve to adequately address the issue and ignite productive dialogue.

RAW conversations are not monologues in which the leader speaks and the other person simply listens and takes note. As a matter of fact, a good leader will ask exploratory questions and then listen intently. Leaders often feel as though they are expected to have the answers and so they speak more often than they listen. But great leaders know how to lead exploratory conversations through the art of asking powerful questions and then listening intently. They don't tell—they inquire. They help others grow by allowing them to come up with their own answers and empowering them to take ownership in finding solutions.

At the same time, these developmental conversations need to be forward-facing. RAW conversations are used to move the dialogue forward, not simply parse the past. Often leaders use coaching conversations to do post-mortem evaluations, dissecting every element of a failed endeavor. This is supposedly done so that mistakes are not repeated. More often than not, though, those involved ruminate on faults and assign blame, casting aspersions on those involved. The only reason to look to the past is for insight, not indictment.

If RAW conversations relate to the past, they do so for the purpose of discussing ideas and methodology, not assassinating persons. Eleanor Roosevelt is often attributed for having said, "Great minds discuss ideas; average minds discuss events; small minds discuss people." For our purposes, I would slightly modify the quote to say, "Powerful conversations explore creative options; poor conversations debate problems; worthless conversations indict people."

3. *Wrestle with solutions.*

RAW conversations work issues through to completion. They take the problem to the mat and stay with it until the problem taps out. In RAW conversations, both parties are committed to staying engaged until there is complete resolution.

Sometimes people prefer a problem they can't solve to a solution that they don't like. They get stuck. A RAW conversation can coach them out of a rut. At other times, poor performance or relational conflict may need to be addressed. Whatever the case, the end result should always be to find a solution to the problem.

> **> Sometimes people prefer a problem they can't solve to a solution that they don't like.**

RAW conversations are not always easy to conduct. At first, those involved may feel like they are entering a tunnel of chaos. But if they stay there long enough, and can conduct themselves with emotional maturity, they will soon begin to see the light at the end of the tunnel. Staying engaged in this process takes boldness and tenacity. But those who are willing to pursue this type of authenticity value both relationships and community to the degree that they refuse to stop short of resolution.

Be forewarned: not all RAW conversations have a positive outcome. The outcome is usually conditioned by the presence of humility and maturity. Humility in that both parties are willing to acknowledge and own whatever part of the problem they can honestly accept. Both parties must be mature enough to handle the conversation in such a way as not to provoke the other or become emotionally volatile. If maturity and humility are both present, then relational harmony and personal growth are often the result of RAW conversations.

The RAW Process

We have spoken about the purpose, so now let's discuss the process of a RAW conversation. Like its purpose, there are three steps in the process.

1. *Reflect reality.*

   Those who initiate the conversation must state, in clear and compelling terms, reality as they see it. Avoidance of any issue will only postpone the inevitable. Remember, reality always shows up. Many times these conversations are akin to a person holding up a mirror so they can see themselves as others do. Each of us has blind spots, and we may not see the negative wake we are leaving in our relational worlds. RAW conversations provide light and insight, showing how we can more effectively move in our relational hemisphere.

2. *Advance the issue.*

   The focus of a RAW conversation must always be to build a brighter future. Relationships are risky. But the people who have the greatest impact on us are those who believe the best *in us*, want the best *for us*, and expect the best *from us*.

   Expecting the best means we don't let one another settle for less than our best. If we are committed to one another, then we owe it to one another to confront when necessary, coach when helpful, and encourage when needed. Advancing means calling out the very best in each other and challenging each other to stretch beyond what we may believe to be the limits of our capability. The desired result of a RAW conversation should always be growth.

3. *Wrestle to resolution.*

Don't jump out of the ring. Stay engaged until the problem is taken to the mat and taps out. If the conversation turns emotional, you may need to postpone the match for a short time. But both parties must commit to not abandoning the process before completion. Completion means you have adequately addressed the issues, found solutions, and the relationship remains intact.

> **❯ Don't settle for conflict management. Stay engaged until you reach a resolution.**

Don't settle for conflict management. Who wants to continue to manage a relationship fraught with conflict? Stay engaged until you reach a resolution. When resolution is properly sought, the issue is clearly identified, candidly discussed, and a commitment has been made to take corrective action. Additionally, resources have been identified to ensure the success of the process. And frequent follow-up should also be a commitment in order to monitor progress.

Preparing for a RAW Conversation

RAW conversations can be challenging. Properly preparing for them is essential to their success. So, now let's look at four elements you must evaluate before engaging in this type of developmental conversation.

Check Yourself

It's important that you approach each conversation with the right motivation. Why do you want to engage in this discussion? If the reason is anything other than to help the other person grow, put the conversation on hold. Sometimes leaders just want to get something off their chest. Maybe they feel like they need to put someone in their place. Or they may just need to vent. None of these are good reasons to have a developmental conversation. RAW conversations should not be punitive. They may eventually include boundaries if certain behaviors do not change, but the hope is for them to be helpful in tone and content. The goal should always be growth and restoration. You should not approach them with any ill will toward the recipient.

Your ego needs to be checked at the door. This is not about making a statement as much as it's an attempt to provide helpful fodder for developmental coaching. If your motivation is right and the conversation is effective, then the end result should be deeper trust, respect, and connection between you and the other individual.

Know Your Audience

If your motivation is right, then the first questions you should ask are: What does this person need from me right now to be more successful? What helpful insight, coaching byte, or reflection would be most advantageous? What is the best way I can help this person grow? This is not merely about what the leader wants in terms of production but rather what needs to be revealed in order to inspire the in-dividual to bring their best to the table.

It would also serve you well to know the emotional state of the person you are engaging in this conversation. Is the timing right? We all deal with struggles occasionally that knock us off-kilter emotionally. Is this a good time to address this topic? Would it be more advantageous to wait until after a particular deadline has passed? What kind of stress is this person under right now? All these are good questions to consider. The content of the conversation may be spot-on, but if the timing is bad, then the impact can easily be lost. Even if the conversation cannot be postponed, at least you can enter into it with sensitivity.

Crystalize the Message

What is the singular point of the conversation? RAW conversations are not conducted in a shotgun fashion. Vague generalities will not provide the kind of clear coaching necessary to curb poor behavior or improve lackluster performance. You must be clear, concise, and compelling in your communication. There is no room for ambiguity. You must know exactly what attitude or behavior needs to be addressed and explore that thoroughly from their perspective.

While there must be a clear point to this encounter, ideally you will get to the point in a masterfully circuitous way. The art of the RAW conversation lies not in the telling but in the asking. Good leaders ask probing and powerful questions to guide the conversation into exploratory waters. These questions lead the other party to greater self-awareness and allow them to take ownership of the change process.

Lead with Questions

People grow into the conversations we create around them. And the best way to start a conversation is to ask great questions. Questions allow the other person to think through and own their answers. Great questions can serve as channel markers, pointing the way to open water and keeping the conversation from running aground.

Through great questions we seek understanding. They provide the opportunity for explanation and exploration. If used effectively, they are nonthreatening yet can lead the way into substantive conversation.

> **❯ People grow into the conversations we create around them. And the best way to start a conversation is to ask great questions.**

For RAW conversations to have the desired impact, it's essential that you have a game plan. Like a coach who knows the game, the field of play, and the opposition, a good leader knows which questions will likely advance the conversation down the field. Questions should be crafted in advance to maximize the opportunity.

Here are just a few questions you can use to ignite a RAW conversation (these are simply examples and may be modified to suit a specific situation):

- What seems to be the biggest challenge you are facing?
- What do you think could be done to enhance collaboration?
- How do you work best?
- Is there anything you could do differently to elevate your performance?
- What processes could we improve?

- If you were in charge, what one thing would you do differently?
- The project seems to be stalling. In your opinion, what are we missing?
- Your performance appears to be slipping. Is there anything I can provide to help you get back on track?
- What are you doing that you wish you weren't?
- What do you wish you were doing that you're not?
- Are you fulfilled in your current role and responsibilities?
- What excites you most about your job/career?
- What, in your opinion, is the problem, and what role can you play in making it right?
- What would it take to engage everyone?
- What inspires you?
- How do you like to be rewarded?
- What skills would you like to learn?
- What would an inspiring culture look like to you?
- What is the biggest problem you are currently trying to solve?
- Are you using your time and energy appropriately?
- How can I best help you?

And be sure to avoid the following questions:

- How do you think things are going?
- Why did this happen?
- Who is to blame for this failure?
- Didn't you have a plan for this?

- What were you thinking?
- Who is causing the problem?
- Do you need me to get involved?

Questions that seek to assign blame, cast aspersions, or remove responsibility from the person being addressed are not helpful. Stick with forward-facing questions that reinforce the fact that ownership of the issue lies squarely with the individual you have engaged in the RAW conversation. Questions should be crafted to help that person assess, diagnose, and take action to rectify the situation.

Now that we have looked at the purpose of and process and preparation for a RAW conversation, it may be helpful to provide a leader's checklist of components that must be in place for a RAW conversation to have full impact.

RAW Conversation Leader's Checklist

___ **Have the conversation in private.** Praise people in public. Provide correction and coaching in private. When you have something good to say about someone, it can be amplified when expressed to the masses. But when you have a challenge or conflict, or there is need for correction, have those conversations in private. As the leader, you want to provide a safe environment to ensure the conversation is productive.

___ **Clarify the issue.** As mentioned previously, clarifying the issue is best done through the use of exploratory questions. By giving the individual the opportunity to process and respond to the question, you are allowing them to gain greater self-awareness. However, if that serves to be unproductive, then you may need to clearly articulate the concerns.

___ **Provide specific examples of the behavior you see that needs to change.** The key here is *what you see*. This cannot be information from a third party or hearsay. You cannot and should not try to speak for someone else. Whether to reinforce the other person's assessment or to clarify your own position, the more clearly you can illustrate the issue, the more helpful it will be.

___ **Describe the emotional impact of the issue.** Every experience in life is emotionally framed. Words and actions have an emotional impact on others. It's the wake that is left behind someone's actions. Sometimes others need to be shown that wake clearly. Often people simply don't slow down long enough to smell their own exhaust. It's important for them to realize how they are impacting the people and environments in which they move.

___ **Clarify what is at risk.** RAW conversations identify what is at stake if corrective action is not taken. If the issue goes unaddressed, then it could have a negative impact on the individual, the team, or the organization at large. If corrective action is not taken, then it may also have repercussions related to future responsibilities and employment options. All of this should be spelled out and a course of action specified.

___ **If appropriate, identify your contribution to the problem.** It may be necessary for you as the leader to acknowledge that part of the problem may have been your responsibility. This is not meant in any way to be disingenuous. If it's not true, don't say it. If you assume responsibility erroneously, it could very likely enable bad behavior. However, if there is reason, then you must own whatever role you may have played in the problem.

___ **Partner to come to resolution.** The pivot point in the conversation is when you offer the resources and emotional support to adequately address the issue. This allows the recipient to know that you are truly on their side and have their best interest at heart. Pointing out the issue isn't enough. Providing the necessary support, coaching, and resources to effectively resolve the issue is what will determine the success of the outcome.

___ **Follow up frequently.** These conversations may fail to produce long-lasting positive change if you are not committed to engage until the process is complete. Periodic checkpoints should be established to monitor progress and ensure that adequate resources are available.

There are several mistakes that leaders commonly make when having these developmental dialogues. The purpose of highlighting these errors is to simply help you avoid these pitfalls. If you want your RAW conversation to have maximum impact, then avoid these missteps:

- *Doing most of the talking.* It's important to be in the moment. After asking great questions, listen intently to the answers and respond accordingly. Remember, this is not a monologue. You should not be doing the majority of the talking if you want the other party to engage in healthy self-evaluation.

- *Asking the wrong questions.* Never start off the conversation with a question like, "So, how do you feel things are going?" If you do, you deserve to hear the response, "Just fine!" Then, where do you go? Try something to the effect of this: "I haven't gotten the feeling that the team is hitting on all cylinders recently. What do you think you could do personally to improve the situation?" Or "We have a problem in that _____. What do you see as the solution?"

- *Taking the Oreo cookie approach.* This is from an old school of thought that correction is best delivered between affirmative statements. It's supposed to soften the blow of the bad news. But people see right through this. If you have invited someone into a conversation to give praise, then give it genuinely. But if this is meant to be a developmental conversation, then get to the point. Don't beat around the bush or attempt to soften your message or it may very well get lost.

- *Machine-gunning.* Addressing too many issues at once will diminish the impact of the conversation. Each conversation should have a single point and purpose. Be laser-focused and make your single point effectively.

- *Sticking to the script.* While it's good to be well prepared and have your questions crafted in advance, be flexible once you get into the conversation. As the dialogue unfolds, it may take you in a totally different direction. Be open. You may find it to be more impactful than you originally hoped if you allow your conversation to take a natural course. By being in the moment, you can adapt your questions and approach to create maximum value.

- *Not checking for feelings.* It may be necessary to stop occasionally and get a read on the other person's emotions. Or you may have to call a time-out yourself if you begin to feel that you are losing control of the direction of the conversation. RAW conversations are frequently filled with heightened emotions. Don't press on if the climate devolves to the point that it becomes nonproductive. You may have to take a break and come back together at a later point. Just make sure you are both committed to continuing the process, and don't let too much time lapse before you reconvene.

- *Coming to a resolution too quickly.* Because these conversations can often be uncomfortable, many people will want to jump out of the ring before the wrestling is complete. If you seek to wrap up the conversation prematurely, then you will inevitably be addressing the issue again. Make sure you both feel you have come to a mutually agreed upon course of action and you can both affirm your commitment to growing your relationship.

- *Assuming the conversation was effective.* Only time will tell the true impact of the RAW conversation. It's imperative that you follow up and follow through on your commitments. Circling back around periodically to check in sends a clear message about the importance of the issue and your willingness to stay engaged in the process.

RAW conversations are not always easy, but they are necessary. If people grow into the conversations that we create around them, then the quality of those conversations will determine the quality and depth of our relationships. Many individuals, teams, and organizations settle for superficial relationships. But healthy people and strong cultures require substantive interpersonal dialogue. RAW conversations are a way that people express a commitment to helping others realize how rare and valuable they are.

Through thoughtful and constructive developmental dialogue, we can help one another grow and mature as individuals and as leaders. But it means we must care enough about someone to leave our comfort zone and risk a relationship for their benefit and growth. Healthy relationships demand that we not settle for conflict management. We must stay engaged until there is conflict resolution. We must have the moral and intestinal fortitude to stay in the tunnel of chaos until we see light.

When approached with openness and humility, RAW conversations can be an extremely impactful tool in a leader's toolbox. When wielded with skill, RAW conversations can lead to personal growth and development and yield highly functioning teams. When done effectively, RAW conversations render performance reviews nothing more than a record of prior developmental conversations, which should be happening continually.

›› GAINING TRACTION: Questions for Consideration & Application

1. How frequently should you be having developmental conversations with your team members and why?

2. What are the three components of a RAW conversation and why is each element important?

3. How should a leader best prepare for a RAW conversation?

4. Why is it important to lead a RAW conversation with questions?

5. What are some common mistakes leaders make when conducting these types of developmental conversations? How can you avoid making the same ones?

TWELVE

RE:SOLUTION

The final forming of a person's character lies in their own hands.

—Anne Frank

Leadership involves far more than garnering a following. It isn't merely getting people to do as you please. Leadership, at its best, is the ability to inspire others to move toward personal maturity so that they may make a positive wake in the world. Leadership is the ability to impart the courage necessary to deal with life honestly and the fortitude to grow beyond limitations. Good leaders force us to face ourselves, believe in ourselves, and, when necessary, change ourselves.

Eleanor Roosevelt once said, "People grow through experience if they meet life honestly and courageously. This is how character is built."[1] The challenge is that many people aren't capable of facing life honestly. Pretense, posturing, and self-protection obscure the path toward growth. As long as someone is trying to promote themselves as being flaw-free, there is little room for growth. Of course, few would willingly acknowledge they are spinning their image in such a way, but their actions defy their false humility. A person who acts defensively and deflects responsibility is trying to mask and cover.

The Four Steps of Growth

It has often been said that growth begins with self-awareness. The ability to either honestly self-assess or have the openness to seriously consider the assessment of another is the beginning of self-knowledge. But growth requires more than simply knowing your strengths, weaknesses, and what you need to work on.

> **The ability to either honestly self-assess or have the openness to seriously consider the assessment of another is the beginning of self-knowledge.**

Growth, to be complete, is a four-step process. Good leaders know this and provide the resources necessary for those they lead to experience each step. Let me innumerate these four steps, as set forth by Dr. Robert Hartman, the modern father of axiology.[2]

1. Know Yourself

It may seem obvious that in order to grow, you need to know yourself. You need to know what makes you tick. You need to be aware of the people and circumstances that energize you and those that drain you. You need to know how to leverage your strengths and mitigate your weaknesses. You certainly benefit from understanding your emotional constitution—comprehending what inspires you to perform at your peak and when you are vulnerable. Based on these statements, you might assume people have a reasonable grasp on the motivational forces that compel them to take the actions they do. You may also assume others have the emotional intelligence to harness and maximize their emotional fluctuations. Both assumptions would be grossly mistaken.

I would venture to say that most people live unexamined lives. Most spend little time in self-reflection or introspection. They do not ask themselves the hard questions regarding the motivations behind their behavior or wrestle long enough with their personal demons to drag them into the daylight. Personal growth is sacrificed on the altar of rationalization. A spirit of defensiveness often deludes developmental fodder. As long as life is *working*, most never stop to address their hypocrisy. So they limp along, partially paralyzed, leaning on the crutch of self-justification.

José Emilio Pacheco, the great Mexican poet, writes, "We are all hypocrites. We cannot see ourselves or judge ourselves the way we see and judge others."[3] We all have blind spots that prevent us from seeing ourselves objectively. That is why we need to be involved in healthy relationships with people who know us well and are bold enough to provide insights. An insight is an understanding that sheds light or helps solve a problem. An insight may also reveal the source of emotional difficulty or provide a glimpse into the motivational forces behind someone's actions, thoughts, or behavior. Insights lead to self-knowledge.

207

Without honest feedback from others, many will simply continue to live in a self-created delusion, unaware of the negative ways in which they are impacting those around them. While profiles and assessments can provide helpful insights, nothing is as beneficial as real-time feedback from those who are closest to you. The key to gleaning transformative insight that leads to personal maturity is one's openness to receiving the feedback offered.

There is a proverb that says, "Faithful are the wounds of a friend who corrects out of love and concern, but the kisses of an enemy are deceitful because they serve his hidden agenda." To have a friend who is so vested in your growth that they would risk the relationship to bring something to your attention is rare. Those who have a relationship of that depth, with even a few people, are truly fortunate. This type of friend truly has your best interest at heart and, at the same time, has your back. They are willing to tell it as they see it when it comes to your character development. But, as I said, this kind of deep friendship is a rare gift. More often than not, you must invite this kind of candid, critical feedback.

The question is, Who in your life has the code to your garage? Who knows where all your emotional junk is neatly stowed away? Who do you allow to rummage around in your trash? Who are you open, authentic, and vulnerable with? Who do you give permission to call your bluff when you are full of yourself? Many people go an entire lifetime without having that type of relationship with anyone. But those who do are among the most self-aware people I know.

If you truly want to experience an exercise in self-knowledge, then work hard to cultivate a few high-trust, totally transparent relationships. Give each of those individuals carte blanche to be completely candid with you when they see you acting in ways that may be harmful to yourself and others. Give them free rein to address the issues without invitation. At first you may have to ask them to give you the last 10 percent, the down-and-dirty feedback that is sometimes hard to deliver. Ask them not to hold back. Invite them to be on your Personal Development Board of Trustees. Trustees are those entrusted with the responsibility to supervise the affairs of an organization. Or call them your coaches, counselors, mentors, or BFFs. The point is that you meet with them regularly and reveal the real you in an effort to seek the insight necessary to lead you to growth and maturity.

Remember, relational maturity is marked by how well you relate to others. And the only way you will truly be able to assess how well you are doing is to see yourself the way others do. You have to seek objective outside input to gain the insight necessary to grow up.

2. Choose Yourself

Choosing one's self may sound like a strange concept. But let me unpack the idea. All of us have people in our lives whom we admire and respect. We may even attempt to emulate them. That is a good thing. However, for many this can easily morph into envy and covetousness. When this happens, a person may feel discontent when they compare their own life to someone else's advantages, successes, possessions, and relationships.

The truth is that many people have an inordinate infatuation with the lives of others, particularly celebrities and athletes. That's why tabloids are so abundant at the grocery store checkout lanes. Print media and reality shows play off this intrigue about the experiences of others. Social media allows us to track the lives of those with whom we have a friendship or a fascination. And if we are not careful, we can find ourselves wasting time wishing we were in their situations rather than focusing on making our own situation better. You've probably been on a social media site and found yourself thinking, *Wow, that's nice! I wish I could* do that, *or* have that, *or* experience that.

Living life vicariously through others is unfulfilling. It will leave you feeling hollow and discontent. Rather than wasting time wishing you were in someone else's shoes, why not cobble a better pair for yourself? Don't long for the life of another. Instead, choose to spend your time and energy to build a better you. As I have told all of my four children, "Choose to be you—everyone else is taken. Be a first-rate version of yourself, not a knock-off of someone else. Spend your time and energy building a better you."

Be inspired by the example of others. But, more importantly, strive to be an example to others that will inspire them to greatness. Choose to invest in yourself.

3. Create Yourself

Once you have chosen yourself, you have to set about the task of creating yourself. Creating yourself means constantly seeking to improve. An attitude of growth is one that says, "Today, I'm better than I was yesterday. But I'm only half as good today as I'll be tomorrow!" Every day is a fresh opportunity to improve. Constantly seek to better your best.

Those with a growth mind-set pursue relationships and seek resources that will enable them to advance toward maturity. They give themselves and others the grace not to be tied to the past and the encouragement to construct a brighter future. Creating one's self is a matter of making a conscious effort to strengthen one's character. This kind of commitment requires one to make a resolution—a wholehearted determination not to settle for anything less than one's best. It is not an attempt to gain perfection, for that's impossible. To posture growth as the pursuit of perfection will only lead to pride and pretense, since perfection is unattainable. Rather, growth is a constant striving toward improvement. This requires both discipline and determination.

Great players practice until they get it right. But champions practice until they can't get it wrong. That is the kind of commitment necessary for the construction of character. It is the demonstration of discipline to repeatedly perform at such a high level that constant improvement becomes second nature.

The creation of character also involves being solution-oriented. Those with character worth cultivating are forward-facing problem-solvers. They do not ruminate on the past. They celebrate victories and learn from failures but never get stuck in a previous era. They may examine the past for insights but never for the purpose of indicting others. They then apply the insights they glean to move toward finding a solution to a problem

> **Those with character worth cultivating are forward-facing problem-solvers.**

or the resolution of a conflict so they can pursue a higher path. That path is one that leads to constant improvement.

4. Give Yourself

Personal growth is not complete until one has positively changed the lives of others. As we learned earlier, self-actualization is not the pinnacle of the pyramid. Self-transcendence, according to Maslow's later writings, should take the top tier on the hierarchy of needs. Self-transcendence means moving beyond simply reaching one's full potential to creating value for others. This value may come in the form of inspiring, coaching, or giving to others through acts of kindness and generosity. It's giving back—and paying it forward. It's investing heavily in the lives of others. It's leaving a positive wake in the world.

Healthy people want to be part of something that transcends themselves. They want to do good for others. They want to leave a legacy. Life, to be meaningful, must be about something more than breathing our share of oxygen and consuming the planet's resources for our own pleasure. Life, at its best, means that the world is left a better place because of our presence. Life is not about having and hoarding. Life, to be relationally rich, means impacting others in a way that somehow makes their story just a little bit better. It is about enriching life through healthy relationships.

Viktor Frankl is a famous Austrian neurologist and psychiatrist who survived four Nazi concentration camps and later went on to write *Man's Search for Meaning*. In that work, the founder of logotherapy expresses the belief that human nature is motivated by the search for a life purpose. That purpose can be found in love and a meaningful existence. He writes, "As to the causation of meaninglessness, one may say, albeit in an oversimplifying vein, that people have enough to live by but nothing to live for; they have the means but no meaning."[4] For Frankl, meaning was found in work (doing something significant), in love (caring for another person), and in courage (finding meaning in suffering).

Logotherapy, then, is about curing the soul by leading it to find meaning in life.[5]

Frankl explains his understanding of how self-actualization and self-transcendence were intertwined when he writes,

> By declaring that man is responsible and must actualize the potential meaning of his life, I wish to stress that the true meaning of life is to be discovered in the world rather than within man or his own psyche, as though it were a closed system. I have termed this constitutive characteristic "the self-transcendence of human existence." It denotes the fact that being human always points, and is directed, to something, or someone, other than oneself—be it meaning to fulfill or another human being to encounter. The more one forgets himself—by giving himself to a cause to serve or another person to love—the more human he is and the more he actualizes himself. What is called self-actualization is not an attainable aim at all, for the simple reason that the more one would strive for it, the more he would miss it. In other words, self-actualization is possible only as a side-effect of transcendence.[6]

Frankl was fond of saying, "The meaning of your life is to help others find the meaning of theirs."[7]

The lesson for leaders here is that if you want people to be energized by their work, then you must help them connect their personal passion and contributions to corporate objectives. If team members do not see how their work connects directly to the overall objectives of the organization, then they can easily become frustrated and begin to feel that their work is meaningless.

Good leaders tap into this innate desire for meaningful work and deeper interpersonal connection and help those under their tutelage connect personal passion with corporate purpose to find fulfillment in their jobs. Healthy people want to make a significant contribution to a worthy cause, whether it's a professional or philanthropic endeavor. They want to know that what they are doing is making a positive difference in the world. They want to be part of something larger than themselves and to leave a legacy of good.

Bringing It Together

Leaders who understand these four steps in the growth process can assist their team members in assessing both where they are and how to advance toward maturity. When we help people grow personally, it pays rich dividends professionally. When we help people grow to be better spouses, parents, coaches, and community leaders, they also become better team members. Leadership is about wanting the best for our people in every aspect of life. And when we have strong team members, they can effectively create an environment of collaboration, where everyone has the opportunity to leverage their passions and strengths to solve problems, elevating both engagement and productivity.

The key to building a highly functioning team is to focus on the individual growth of each team member. Maturity is the antidote for a dysfunctional team. The more leaders invest in helping their team members grow, the greater the team's synergy. Leaders do not merely garner followers. Leaders engage others in the growth process. And as others grow, they will be inclined to follow those who are committed to their personal development. Leaders must make a resolution to invest heavily in the growth and development of their team members. At the same time, they must be committed to work through interpersonal conflict until there is resolution. Meeting corporate objectives and managing metrics are not enough to engender loyalty and discretionary effort. People's passions are ignited when they are deeply connected relationally, find meaning and purpose in their work, and are engaged in a personal growth process, which gives them a sense of self-mastery.

>> **GAINING TRACTION: Questions for Consideration & Application**

1. If growth begins with self-awareness, what can you do to become more self-aware as a leader?

2. How many people have the "code to your garage," and how often do you seek their advice and counsel on significant matters? Describe a situation in which seeking counsel proved beneficial.

3. In what ways are you seeking to create a better self?

4. How are you giving of yourself to others? What impact is that having on you? What impact is that having on others?

5. What are some steps outlined in this chapter that are necessary in order for character development to take place?

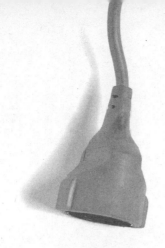

REIMAGINE LEADERSHIP:
SUSTAINABILITY

THIRTEEN

LEADERSHIP BEYOND SELF-INTEREST

I don't know what your destiny will be, but one thing I do know: the only ones among you who will be really happy are those who have sought and found how to serve.

—Albert Schweitzer

As the story goes, a young man bought a horse from a farmer for $250 and arranged to get the animal the following day. The next morning, the farmer arrived at the young man's house and said, "Sorry, son, but I have some bad news. Your horse died last night."

"That's all right," the young man said. "Just give me back my money."

"Well, I can't rightly do that seein' as I've already gone out and spent it all and fact bein' she became yours when you bought 'er yesterday," replied the farmer.

The young man said, "Okay, then just bring me back the dead horse."

Curious, the farmer asked, "Whatcha gonna do with a dead horse?"

"I'm going to raffle 'er off."

"You're joshin'! You can't raffle off a dead horse," the old man said.

"Why, sure I can," said the whippersnapper. "I just won't tell anybody that the horse is dead."

Several weeks later, the farmer ran into the young man in town and asked what had happened with the raffle and dead horse. With a Cheshire-cat grin on his face, he leaned in to the old farmer and said, "I did what I said I was going to do. I sold five hundred tickets for five dollars apiece and made a profit of $2,245 after backing out my loss to you."

The farmer appeared puzzled. "Well, didn't anyone complain about the horse being dead?"

"Nobody knew but the guy who won the raffle. When he got upset about the horse being dead, I just gave him his five dollars back."

They say the same young man is now a member of Congress.

The young man was cunning, deceiving others to extract value through his equine ruse. Some may praise him for being shrewd in recovering his losses, but he was nothing more than a charlatan. In retelling the story, I am not attempting to cast aspersions on political leaders in general. I know many public servants at various levels of government who serve the public well and are individuals of stellar character.

Unfortunately, there is a stereotype that far too many politicians serve out of self-interest or on behalf of special interest groups. And every stereotype is founded on some semblance of truth. Partisan politics and bureaucracy create little value. Those who are inclined to do so may use the system to serve themselves and abuse others in the process. What is true in politics is also true in business. Self-serving leaders create little value for their constituents.

The ranks of corporate circles are filled with individuals who demonstrate edgy business acumen, have charismatic personalities, and know how to strategically align people and resources to garner good returns for shareholders. But far too many produce those returns by raffling off whatever it is they are hawking. They extract time and talent from those who have been enlisted to serve their "cause," all while offering the hope of greater returns for those who have invested to make it possible. Many of these executives know how to turn a profit, but often few others beside themselves benefit from their endeavors. Should the organization begin to wane in its vitality, many are prone to pull the cord and float away with a golden parachute, leaving everyone else to deal with a dead horse.

The good news is that there is a growing sense of corporate responsibility and an increasing number of leaders who serve beyond themselves. More and more leaders are returning to solid ethical practices as well as embracing social and environmental responsibility. Organizations are holding leaders more accountable, and the best are those who recognize and reward the contributions of their team members by allowing them to share in the profits that their efforts have produced. Chobani Yogurt is just one example of a company that has done right by their people.

The Chobani Story

According to their website, Chobani is committed to the planet and its people. At Chobani, they believe business can be a force for good and living their guiding mission of better food for more people extends far beyond their products. From humane treatment of cows on their dairy farms to responsible manufacturing practices to being active members of the communities in which they live and work, they are passionate about democratizing good and helping to accelerate universal wellness. One of their priorities is to help small companies with big hearts and ideas challenge the food industry, improving broken systems and making a positive difference. The Chobani Foundation exists to strengthen the communities they call home, improve childhood nutrition and wellness nationally, and help those in need wherever they may live.[1]

Hamdi Ulukaya is the owner, founder, chairman, and CEO of Chobani. Originally from a small dairy-farming community in Turkey, he immigrated to the United States in 1994 to study English and take a few business courses. With the encouragement of his father, he started a modest feta cheese factory in 2002. Three years later, he took a major risk in purchasing a large, defunct yogurt factory that had been closed by Kraft Foods in South Edmeston, New York. It was located in a region that used to be the center of the dairy and cheese industry. By 2012, Chobani had become the world's leading yogurt brand. Due in no small part to the popularity of the brand, the market share for Greek-style yogurt in the US grew from less than 1 percent in 2007 to more than 50 percent in 2013. Ernst & Young named Ulukaya the World Entrepreneur of the Year in 2013.[2]

According to Ulukaya, higher wages for workers lead to greater corporate success. He promotes not only the position that companies can succeed when they pay their workforce more but also that they have a moral obligation to do so. According to Ulukaya, "For the sake of our communities and our people, we need to give other companies the ability to create a better life for more people."[3]

In an interview with Ernst & Young global chairman and CEO Mark Weinberger, Ulukaya said business leaders should promote a sense of purpose in their corporate culture to create a climate of positive change in business and the world. He shared the firm conviction that companies should focus on humanity and not just on their bottom lines. "Business is still the strongest, most effective way to change the world," Ulukaya told Weinberger.[4]

Since the establishment of Chobani, Ulukaya has given 10 percent of his company's net profits to charitable causes and to individuals and organizations dedicated to working toward positive, long-lasting change. In April 2016, he gave his employees a 10 percent share of the enterprise, announcing, "How we built this company matters to me, but how we grow it matters even more and I want you not only to be a part of this growth—I want you to be the driving force of it. To share in our success, to be rewarded by it. . . . This isn't a gift; it's a mutual promise to work together with a shared purpose and responsibility. To continue to create something special and of lasting value."[5]

Ulukaya is compelled by a deep sense of passion and purpose.[6] He is committed to utilizing his resources to work with refugees around the globe, alleviate suffering and hunger, and strengthen the communities in which Chobani has a presence by providing gainful employment. His wake is immense, and his legacy will be long lasting because it rises above self.

When it comes to communicating his company's values to the world, Ulukaya is passionate. His advice? "Just be real." Perhaps it sounds overly simplified, but when a company treats its employees, customers, and community with respect, it's not so difficult.[7]

Grounded Leadership

Leadership must be about something beyond self-interest, greater than self-promotion, and more noble than self-service. Leadership, at its best, has several essential qualities that constitute what I call a *grounded leader*. The term *grounded* refers to someone who is emotionally mature and stable, firmly rooted in convictions and steadfast in determination. Someone who is grounded is practical. Grounded leaders deal in reality and are fully dedicated to garnering significant results. They are also heavily relationally focused and see their role as one that empowers others. Grounded individuals have a profound sense of rootedness because they are comfortable with who they are and act from their core values. Thus, they are not easily swayed by the winds of popular opinion, but live their lives with the mission to serve a noble cause.

> **Leadership must be about something beyond self-interest, greater than self-promotion, and more noble than self-service.**

Let's look at the characteristics of a grounded leader and parse out those qualities that make them so influential.

Rooted in Reality

Grounded leaders operate in truth. They have the capacity to analyze issues and situations objectively. Truth is what it is. They have a keen awareness of what is. They don't allow themselves to be heavily influenced by those who spin, hedge, or twist the truth. They have a deep sense of conviction and trust their intuition. They are discerning and able to separate fact from fiction. They don't jump to conclusions but watch circumstances unfold with keen perception and then deal with each situation according to its merits.

They know that whoever is able to most accurately describe and address reality will emerge the leader, whether or not they were designated. Therefore, they don't deal in half-truths or allow themselves to get swept away by the current of politics. Nor do they become distracted in the court of popular opinion. They call things as they see them and do so with grace and sensitivity. They do not engage in petty debate, knowing that arguments never settle differences. They simply speak the truth and let the consequences take their course. They do not force their will on others or attempt to manipulate people or situations to meet their agenda. They speak and act decisively. They influence others because they garner the trust that comes from aligning themselves with the truth.

They are mature enough to realize that reality always shows up.

And when it does, those who have recognized and addressed it appropriately will influence others significantly. While some may attempt to interpret or twist the truth to conform to their self-serving agendas, grounded leaders align themselves with the truth to serve others. They do what is right and speak what is true. Consistently.

Emotionally Centered

Grounded leaders operate from the core of who they are. They are committed to their values and convictions. They remain true to themselves and do not morph to match their environment. They are not chameleons. They are emotionally healthy, balanced, and centered. They are centered in the sense that their perception of reality and their response to it revolve around an axis of deep, personal values. Grounded leaders are solid and secure in who they are and what they believe, so their values govern their behavior. They are balanced and emotionally healthy in that they neither suppress their emotions nor allow their emotions to hijack their capacity for reasoning. Their emotions alert them to potential danger or enhance their perceptions, but they do not dictate their understanding of reality. Rather, grounded leaders combine reason with the reflective capacity to gain insight from each emotional reaction in order to respond appropriately.

In other words, grounded leaders demonstrate a high degree of emotional intelligence. They are masters when it comes to understanding their own feelings and are deeply empathetic to the feelings of others. This ability to sense and interpret emotions in a mature way allows them to feel deeply with others while interpreting and harnessing their own emotions in productive ways. No matter how intense a situation may become, they do not shut down or withdraw emotionally. Nor do they let their emotions run amuck. Because grounded leaders have mastered the ability to harness their emotions, they can

> › **Because grounded leaders have mastered the ability to harness their emotions, they can remain clearheaded, calm, and in control.**

remain clearheaded, calm, and in control. This serves the grounded leader well in navigating even the stormiest relational seas. Ultimately, their values serve as the keel, running deep and keeping them upright and afloat, even in rough relational waters and against strong emotional gales.

Relationally Rich

Grounded leaders put a premium on healthy relationships. They understand that helping others grow toward maturity is the highest priority of living in community. This community begins in the home and works itself out through the concentric circles of family, friends, colleagues, and acquaintances. Grounded leaders move in their relational spheres, influencing and encouraging others by their example of open, honest, and transparent living.

Those who are grounded have learned how to address and resolve conflict effectively. They do not settle for simply managing differences by sweeping them under the carpet. Nor do they engage in counterproductive debate. Instead, they speak with truth and grace. They are not unnerved by tension but realize it can sometimes be healthy, forcing both parties to reconsider their positions and come to a mutual understanding. They know that the healthiest relationships are not conflict-free. But relationships in which both parties have dealt with and resolved conflict well produce growth for all involved.

Beyond seeking resolution to relational conflict, grounded individuals are also quick to forgive. They know that holding a grudge is not beneficial. Once issues are resolved, they release them emotionally and do not let them hinder progress in the relationship.

Those who are grounded also have both a depth and breadth of relationships. These relationships serve to sharpen them and allow them to invest in the growth and development of others in a way that is mutually beneficial. They know relationship catalyzes growth, so they invest heavily in moving their relationships toward maturity. Sometimes this happens through casual conversation. Sometimes it takes the form of a mentoring relationship. Sometimes it's more directive, as in a coaching conversation with a direct report. Or it may be a disciplinary conversation in which acceptable boundaries are established. Whatever the case, grounded leaders recognize that people grow into the conversations that are created around them and are conscious of building healthy relationships through substantive conversations.

Results-Oriented

Another key characteristic of grounded leaders is that they can be counted on to get the job done. They possess the drive and determination that lead to accomplishment. While they are relationally rich, they are also intent on doing good for others and making a difference. This means they thrive on collaboration and are energized by rallying resources and people to do a job well. They have experienced the satisfaction that comes from being able to synergize people to accomplish more collectively than they ever could have individually.

Grounded leaders are resourceful and responsible. They demonstrate a high degree of competence and evoke confidence among those they lead. They are consistent and can be counted on to follow through to completion.

Others-Focused

Grounded leaders are servant leaders. They see their role as one that serves others, often in a self-sacrificial way. They understand that the way to success is to make those around them successful. And that all the good they want in life is a by-product of creating value for others.

Their life and leadership are rooted in the fact that fulfillment and satisfaction are found in seeking to produce value for others rather than extracting value for self. Therefore, grounded leaders always take into consideration what the other person may need from them in any given situation. They make a conscious effort to create the greatest value for all involved in each situation.

Mission-Minded

Grounded people don't simply have a mission—they are on a mission. They live on purpose, for a purpose, and with purpose. They have a deep desire to leave a positive wake of good in the world. They are keenly aware that the greatest contribution they can make may be found not in what they do but rather in how they do it. Regardless of what vertical or industry they find themselves in, they impact lives positively by simply living and leading in such a way that they seek to make the lives of those around them just a little better.

> **> Grounded leaders always take into consideration what the other person may need from them in any given situation.**

Grounded leaders know that life is bigger than self. They want to leave a mark that cannot easily be erased. So, they give when others take. They notice what others ignore. They engage when others simply walk on by. They spread kindness. They inspire hope. They create value for everyone they encounter. And they encourage everyone else to do the same.

❯❯ GAINING TRACTION: Questions for Consideration & Application

1. What does it mean to be emotionally centered?

2. How can a leader balance being relationally rich with being results-oriented?

3. Who would you say is the most mission-minded leader you have known? Why was that person's leadership impactful to you?

4. Why is it important to be others-focused as a leader? When a leader is not focused on others, what does their leadership style look like?

5. Craft a leadership legacy statement that captures your heart and expresses what you consider to be the purpose of your leadership. It should explain "why" you do what you do.

FOURTEEN

CLOSING THE
REVOLVING DOOR

When we seek to discover the best in others, we somehow
bring out the best in ourselves.

—William Arthur Ward

A war is currently being waged for talent. Good team members may be hard to come by, but leaders understand how critical they are in building strong organizations. The fastest way to enhance culture is to hire top-tier talent whose values align with those of the organization. Conversely, the quickest way to destroy a good culture is to hire the wrong people. As we have said, people are not an organization's greatest resource. The

232

right people are the greatest resource. The *wrong people* are the greatest liability. The cost of a bad hire is much greater than missing out on someone good. It's a conundrum as to why so many organizations hire in a haphazard way or simply do not understand the nuances of attracting top talent.

If an organization wants remarkable results, they must do two things well: (1) hire *remarkable people* and (2) craft a *remarkable culture*. If they do these two things well, then everything else will be much easier. But if they fail on these two points, then everything they attempt to do will become that much more difficult.

The reality is that when you hire remarkable people and place them in a less-than-remarkable culture, they may have a positive impact and elevate the culture. But if they become frustrated and have little hope of making a significant impact, then they easily become disenchanted and leave the organization. Similarly, if you have a stellar culture but hire less-than-remarkable people, then those who do not embrace the culture can quickly sour their fellow team members and curb their enthusiasm. Hiring the right people is absolutely critical, yet so many organizations do a poor job when it comes to selecting talent. Consequently, turnover is high, morale is low, and momentum is diminished.

Organizations that do not put a heavy emphasis on the acquisition of top-tier talent will forever be plagued by low morale and moderate levels of engagement, accompanied by a frustrated workforce and high attrition.

Let's look at a few elements that diminish the effectiveness of hiring practices and discuss possible solutions.

Why We Stink at Hiring

Part of the problem in identifying top-tier talent in any pool of applicants is simply speed to hire. When a position is vacant, many hiring managers are charged to fill that position as quickly as possible. They often receive bonuses based on minimizing the time that a particular position is empty. As a result, speed takes precedence over substance. Candidates are not thoroughly vetted, the courtship process is truncated, interviews are minimized, and concern for values alignment placed on the back burner.

This, of course, all leads to a lack of transparency for both the candidate and the organization. The candidate is not given time to explore the organization's culture, and the organization does not take the time to connect deeply with the candidate. Assumptions are made and conclusions are drawn that do not reflect reality on either side. Therefore, often a sense of disconnectedness or disillusionment persists when the individual comes on board. Both the organization and the individual have to adjust their expectations. A better alternative would be to simply slow the hiring process to ensure that all parties have a thorough understanding of one another and that there is a culture and values match.

I have a friend who was in a senior-level role at a multinational company with offices in Atlanta. He grew increasingly frustrated that the company he was working for had not been altogether candid about the organizational culture when they were courting him. After several years of enduring a values misalignment, he finally came to terms with the fact that he had wed himself to an organization he could no longer serve effectively. So, he decided to make a transition.

Another company was nearby that he had always admired. Its brand was strong and the culture was the cornerstone on which its founder had built a thriving business. The company was a highly acclaimed leader in its industry. The problem, however, was that the organization had a corporate culture of internal promotion and rarely looked outside to fill open positions. Nevertheless, a position became available that he felt he would be suited to fill, so he threw his name in the hat for consideration at Chick-fil-A.

Eighteen weeks and thirty-six interviews later, he was offered the position. You may think of that as overkill. A process that lengthy and laborious is definitely exhaustive. But that is the point. And it's a common occurrence at Chick-fil-A. You see, my friend was required to interview with every person he would directly touch in the course of his responsibilities. All thirty-six. And some of those interviews lasted for three and a half hours. In the end, they were all required to sign off on his hire. It's safe to say he was thoroughly vetted to make sure he was a good match for the company's culture. At Chick-fil-A, culture is the single most important differentiating factor. In fact, the company is most widely known for its culture—a culture that both attracts and keeps top talent. Chick-fil-A hires first and foremost for culture match and values alignment.

The wisdom in this hiring practice is that it ensures the success of each member of the team. Because everyone who interacts with each new hire is required to give a thumbs-up means they are all committing themselves to provide the support, encouragement, and direction needed for the new team member to be successful. Should relationships become stressed, no one can go passive-aggressive and claim not to have been in support of the hire. Instead, each person has a vested interest to ensure that person is productive. Should that new team member drop out for any reason, it's considered a failure for the entire team. It would mean either that person was not properly vetted or adequate resources were not provided for them to become a productive, contributing team member.

Since many people spend as much time at work as they do with their spouse, it would seem to be common sense not to limit yourself to speed dating before "wedding" yourself to an organization. But I can assure you that common sense is not commonly practiced when it comes to hiring.

Another common mistake is hiring for competency without assessing character. While competency allows you to determine whether someone has the skill set to get the job done, character tells you why and how that person will do the work. Education, previous work experience, endorsements, and testing can help ascertain if someone possesses the knowledge and skills necessary to be productive. But only time will reveal someone's character.

People today are adept at the interview process. They can make a great first impression and easily grasp an understanding of an organization's mission and values simply by perusing a website. However, a considerable amount of time and effort is required to peel back the personal layers and reveal the core of a person. Yet nothing is more important in the pre-hire assessment process than gaining an understanding of someone's value construct. Someone's values serve as the motivational force behind both their beliefs and their behavior. If a clear sense of values alignment between the individual and the organization is not present, then there is sure to be a conflict of values, which will result in lack of unity, poor relational connectedness, and limited productivity. There's a saying that goes, "Hire character; train skill."

Values help us understand what motivates an individual's performance. By values, I am not merely referring to ethical values, although that is part of each person's construct. I am also referring to functional values, or what valuation a person may place on certain critical elements that would lend themselves to productivity and emotional balance. Optimism, perseverance, resilience, self-regard, and role satisfaction all play a significant part in determining whether someone can perform at a high level in a sustainable fashion. This type of information is hard to come by in a behavioral interview process.

Behavioral interviews are conducted on the premise that a person's past accomplishments are predictive of future success. Therefore, by asking the right questions about how the individual has addressed particular issues in the past, the interviewer can get a glimpse as to whether that person will be successful in similar settings in the future. The challenge is that while someone may very well describe a preferred behavior, the interviewer has little opportunity to determine whether the one being interviewed has the emotional health or values construct to actually act on what they recognize to be the most beneficial course of action. They may know the right answer, but will they do the right thing?

> **> Values help us understand what motivates an individual's performance.**

Likewise, rational intelligence testing and personality-based instruments provide little predictive value when it comes to ascertaining the likelihood of someone's long-term success. Traits and tendency tools may show someone's preferred response to specific situations. But a more beneficial approach is to determine someone's values construct through the use of an axiological instrument.

Axiology is the study of values and value creation. It's a strain of philosophy that explores the impact of values on thought processes, decision-making, and, ultimately, performance. The theory is that values form the foundation for all human motivation. People will act in accordance with what they deem will create the greatest value for themselves and others, depending on their orientation. A person's values reveal their worldview, which is a powerful predictor of performance. Because how we view things ultimately drives how we do things. A values-based instrument can provide significant insight into how individuals view themselves and the world around them, as well as how they are likely to interact with others.[1]

Slowing the hiring process to ensure there is a character and chemistry match between the organization and the candidate is as important, if not more important, as making sure they are competent enough to fill the role. A values alignment and culture match is imperative. Hiring top talent is crucial to any organization's success. Your people will ultimately determine the quality of your brand. Remember, the right people are the key to your success. If you get the people and culture pieces right, then everything else is pretty easy. But if you do not, then I can assure you that everything else you do will be much more difficult. Make sure you get your hiring practices right.

> **Remember, the right people are the key to your success. If you get the people and culture pieces right, then everything else is pretty easy.**

Invest for Growth

Organizations invest heavily in product development and process refinement. A lot of thought, effort, and resources are poured into offering a high-quality product that garners market attention. Manufacturing and supply distribution processes are constantly tweaked, eliminating waste and making operations more efficient. A great deal of time and energy are expended in quality control and supply chain management to constantly elevate the brand.

What is fascinating to me is how many organizations invest so little in developing their people. Ultimately, people are the greatest reflection of your brand. No matter how great your product or how efficient your processes, if your people do not interact with the customer in a way that engenders healthy relationships and stellar customer service, then all is for naught.

Two of my children presented a strong appeal to upgrade their phones just before the holiday season. The costs associated with the coveted telecommunications devices teetered on insanity. Parenthetically, I have to tell you that I relish conversations with them describing life before mobile devices. I find great amusement in their responses when I describe the days when mobile meant you could stretch the phone cord into the living room. Nonetheless, I succumbed to their pleas of feigned desperation. Fortunately, I did at least have the

> **> No matter how great your product or how efficient your processes, if your people do not interact with the customer in a way that engenders healthy relationships and stellar customer service, then all is for naught.**

foresight to negotiate the phones to be their Christmas presents from my wife and me.

Though I thought I was adequately prepared, I still experienced sticker shock when they rang up the total for the two phones. I experienced momentary paralysis in my right arm when the salesperson asked for my credit card. But I prevailed and walked out of the store pleased with the fact that I had purchased their phones four weeks before Christmas. Shopping early for holidays and special occasions is not my preferred method of operation.

On Christmas morning, they were both ecstatic when they unwrapped their tiny boxes. But the excitement quickly faded for my daughter when she realized the phone I had purchased for her did not have the camera lens she had wanted. I was dismayed because I had been precise with the sales associate, describing in detail exactly the specifications my daughter had given me and was assured this was the phone she was requesting. Now, granted, I am a technological neophyte, but I assumed the salesperson knew what he was talking about. At least he certainly presented himself as being knowledgeable. And he assured me that she could return it if she wasn't satisfied.

"No problem," I told her. "We can just return it and get the one you had your heart set on."

But when I called the store to explain the situation, I discovered that there was a problem. Evidently, buried in the small print of the twenty-plus-page sales agreement was a clause stipulating that, if not satisfied, the phone could only be returned within a thirty-day window. Well, that was problematic since I had purchased the phones four weeks before Christmas. Nevertheless, I was confident we could work something out with the provider that had sold me the phone. First, I had been a customer of that particular carrier for twenty-plus years. Second, the sales associate had obviously not been informed about product features and had clearly misled me. So, I strode back into the store to make the exchange. I wasn't looking for a refund. I actually wanted to make an exchange for a more expensive phone.

So as not to bore you and to prevent another near stroke for me, I will spare you the details. But I am sure you can imagine. I got the proverbial runaround. I ran more circles than a hamster on a wheel chasing a suspended carrot. The people at the local store were less than helpful and turned more belligerent each time I stated the logic of my position and made an additional appeal. After all, how was I to exchange a present that hadn't been opened by its recipient before the deadline? I calmly escalated my case as high as possible up the corporate ranks. Each person was less and less helpful. With no personal contact, what did they care? When they hung up the phone, they did not have to face me. In the end, those in customer service and their customer loyalty division remained steadfast, referring to the microscopic print on page fourteen of the sales agreement. After having me as a faithful customer for twenty years, they lost me. I chose to move to another carrier.

Now, to be fair, I should have read the sales agreement. But I doubt I am the only person who has ever forgone that mind-numbing exercise. And it was not really the small print that was the straw that broke the camel's back. It was actually the way I was treated by the frontline folks in the store and those whose sole purpose for existence is supposedly to retain long-tenured customers. They were rude. They did not express empathy. Nor did they reflect any remorse. If their hands were tied, then fine. But they at least could have tried to relate to the absurdity of my plight and attempted to console me in my frustration. I had just spent nearly $1,000 on a phone that nobody wanted!

I have reflected on that situation numerous times over the past several months and still cannot wrap my head around it. This is a multinational company. They have state-of-the-art technology, just like everyone else. They have agreements with their providers to which they are bound. I get it. But what they lacked was substantial investment in their people. They had failed to provide adequate training for their team members. Those who interacted with customers were neither knowledgeable about product features and benefits nor well versed on the details of the sales agreement. I had been misled on both fronts. And not just by a single person. More importantly, they were relationally inept. They had no idea how to appropriately address a disgruntled customer. Or they just did not care. They did not adequately understand that their frontline folks are major contributors in building the brand, so the brand became tarnished in my eyes. And they lost a long-time customer!

When organizations fail to invest heavily in their people, they run a substantial risk. Top-tier companies understand how important it is to view their employees as brand ambassadors. They make substantial investments in the training and development of their talent. And that training is not merely based on increasing industry knowledge. They invest to help their people grow in every dimension of life. They know that if they can help them become better spouses, parents, coaches, and community leaders, then they will also become better and more productive team members.

Invest in your people so heavily that they become equipped to go anywhere and be successful. And love them so deeply that they would never want to leave. Then you will have a workforce that will strengthen your brand in the market and engender customer loyalty. Take care of your people and they will take care of your customers. Your customers will appreciate a respite from the hamster wheel and your team members will refrain from exiting through the revolving door.

> **Take care of your people and they will take care of your customers.**

Keeping Your Customers

Many companies struggle with client turnover in the same way they have a hard time holding on to good talent. If you want to retain your most valuable clients and create an allegiance among those you serve, then invest in them heavily and love them deeply. Investing heavily means spending the time necessary to get to know them well. And loving them deeply simply refers to making the effort to anticipate and meet their needs. The more deeply connected you are relationally with your customers, the more likely they are to stick around.

Horst Schulze is a name synonymous with stellar customer service. Most everyone knows him as the man who defined the luxury hotel experience through his long tenure as president of the Ritz-Carlton Hotel Company. As CEO of the Capella Hotel Group, he crafted a new category of service known as ultra-luxury.

One morning over breakfast, I asked Horst to explain the components of the ultra-luxury experience. His answer was so simple that it surprised me. According to Horst, people are looking for three things when they purchase a product or service. If you can deliver on these three expectations, then you can produce a quality experience people will want to repeat. Here are the three things you must remember if you truly want to engender loyalty among those you serve.

1. Don't Make People Wait

Under Horst Schulze's leadership, the Capella brand has adapted to the changing demands of the luxury customer. Revealing an interesting insight about the customer experience, he said, "When we opened our first Ritz-Carlton in 1984, we knew when customers checked in they didn't want to wait longer than four minutes. . . . Now it's become 20 seconds."[2] People do not like to wait; they grow impatient. You do not have to immediately meet their every need, but they do want someone to quickly acknowledge their presence. Whether they are putting their name in at a restaurant hostess station or asking for assistance on a phone call, people want some form of personal interaction. And the sooner you make the relational connection the better.

Few things are more frustrating than placing a call for help only to be greeted by an impersonal message requiring you to respond by pressing one of nine options on your touch screen. Then having to repeat the same process multiple times before you are connected to a breathing being. If you want to create raving fans, then be responsive. Return phone calls and emails promptly. Even if you do not have an answer or cannot resolve an issue immediately, let them know that their question or concern is a priority and that you are working on it.

Silence is deadly. If there is a vacuum in communication, people will often assume the worst. Communicate with your customer base quickly, regularly, and proactively. Acknowledge their presence and concerns. Empathize with them even if you cannot change the situation. The key is to simply be understanding and responsive.

2. Offer a Consistent, Defect-Free Product, and Make It Personal

People don't expect perfection. What they do want is a comfortable and predictable experience. If they buy a bottle of water, it doesn't have to be significantly different from all the other bottled water in the market. It just needs to be cold and the container free from leaks. Consistency is the key.

If a company has multiple locations, it's critical that the brand experience be the same regardless of locale. People want to know what they can expect and have their experience be congruent with those expectations. According to Schulze, "A brand is a promise, and when you start making exceptions, you stop keeping the promise to the customer."[3]

While offering a consistent and defect-free product seems rather mundane, what makes the experience exceptional is the insistence on making it personal. Team members trained by Horst Schulze will do whatever is necessary to deliver what the customer wants—as long as it's not illegal, immoral, or unethical. They are taught to anticipate a customer's need and do everything within their power to seek to meet that need. They are also given the freedom to use their better judgment to make the customer experience memorable. Schulze thinks it is immoral to hire people to fulfill functions. "A chair serves a function. We hire people to join us and be a part of a vision; their function is incidental. We hire human beings to be a part of a dream and to pursue a purpose," Schulze says.[4]

3. Be Kind

Capella hotels are superior because the company hires people to work in an environment defined by belonging and purpose. It fosters a climate in which team members can deliver what the customer wants. Team members must have the freedom to do what is right in each situation and be trusted to use their best judgment. This requires superior knowledge and real leadership at every level throughout the organization, not only management. Capella does not just hire managers—it grooms leaders.

Kindness is the result of anticipating and responding to someone's needs. It's a hallmark of leadership. Horst smiled as he recounted the story of a night bellman who went with a guest to the hospital. It turned out the guest had appendicitis. The bellman stayed with him throughout the night to make sure he was cared for adequately. Such behavior is a reflection of the heart. And it is that kind of heart that sets an organization apart.

"We may not always be immediately present. And occasionally our offerings may not be defect-free. But one thing we can consistently provide is kindness," Schulze told me. When referring to customer service, these words are more valuable than apples of gold in baskets of silver.

>> GAINING TRACTION: Questions for Consideration & Application

1. Why do so many organizations find it difficult to attract and retain top talent?

2. What could you do to improve the hiring practices of your organization?

3. What percentage of your time, resources, and energy go toward investing in your people, as opposed to processes and product? Do you think this allotment of resources is adequate to accelerate growth? Explain your answer.

4. Do you agree with the statement "If you take care of your people, they will take care of your customers"? Why or why not?

5. In what ways could you invest in your people more wisely to garner better customer service?

6. What key factors do you believe could slow or shut the revolving door of talent within your organization?

7. What are the elements of ultra-luxury customer service?

FIFTEEN

LEADING WITH LOVE

To add value to others, one must first value others.

—John C. Maxwell

n *Star Wars: The Last Jedi*, Rose Tico, a young pilot in the Resistance, saves fellow fighter Finn from certain death as he speeds his rickety craft on a suicidal course to destroy a massive First Order battering ram aimed at their last fortified retreat. At the last second, Rose swoops in and diverts Finn from imminent disaster, sending both of their crafts into crash landings. Jumping from his mangled pile of metal, Finn rushes to check on Rose, who has crashed nearby. As Finn pulls the injured Rose from her crushed cockpit, he asks her why she averted him from his mission. She offers a soft and profound revelation.

"We're going to win this war," she says, "not by fighting what we hate but by saving what we love."[1]

It's a poignant moment and a beautiful sentiment.

At times, saving what we love means fighting what we hate. To stand by idly and not respond when the welfare of another is compromised is not acting in a loving manner. Injustice and abuse must be confronted for the destructive forces they are. But more often than not, leading with love is a far more powerful proposition. Love trumps hate.

Love is one of those words that gets thrown around so much that it needs explanation. There is a difference between saying "I love my wife" and "I love hot dogs." The word *love* does not carry quite the same meaning or degree of intensity in the second sentence as it does in the first. Honey, if you are reading this, I promise my love for hot dogs is not even remotely close to the love I have for you!

So, for our purposes, let me define *love* in the context of business relationships. Love simply means we have another person's best interest at heart. Or, as we have noted in our definition of what makes a remarkable culture, we *want the best for one another*. But it's more than simply wanting or wishing the best for someone. It's taking action to ensure the best becomes a reality. So, when it comes to actionable items, let me offer a few tangible ways in which you can express love for those around you.

Share Your Time

Time is a language of love. When we take time with someone, it demonstrates that they are important. One of the most valuable resources any of us has is our time. And when we take the time to invest in others, we are showing them that they matter to us. But because time is such a precious commodity, we must be judicious and intentional with it.

I am not talking about wasting time shooting the breeze. Few of us can afford that. I am talking about slowing down enough so that we become sensitive to the opportunities to invest our time wisely in our team members. A word of encouragement spoken at just the right time, when a colleague or direct report is struggling with a difficult task, can be immensely uplifting. Expressing, in the moment, appreciation for an expenditure of discretionary effort can fuel performance.

Sometimes simply being present, without saying a word, in times of tragedy can make a profound statement of support and engender loyalty. When my wife lost her younger sister to a sudden illness, the CEO of her company drove three hours to attend the funeral service. The chapel was overflowing with friends and family members to the point that he, along with other team members, had to stand along the wall. The service was an emotional blur and the receiving lines before and after the service were lengthy. I don't think he even had the opportunity to address the family that day. But his presence was felt. It was a silent but profound show of support. He cared. He was present.

Another way to give time is through coaching and mentoring. It's imperative that leaders give helpful feedback in a personal way. I was speaking with a frustrated leader recently who was bemoaning the fact that there had been a shuffling of the deck chairs within his organization and his new supervisor lacked the relational qualities of the previous leader. When a major initiative was launched, it was necessary to establish clear direction to ensure that the project stay on course. When he asked for some personal time with his supervisor to discuss the critical issues they were facing, he got what had grown to be her standard response. His superior simply said, "I don't have time to discuss this. Just put your points in an email and send them to me. I will get back to you with my thoughts."

Her response left this leader to interpret his boss's request in one of two ways. Either the boss thought, *The project isn't important enough to warrant my personal attention* or *You are not important enough to warrant my attention.* If the first option was the case, then why should it warrant the leader's attention? The possibility of either option left him stifled. Like a sailboat sitting idly with its mainsheet luffing in the wind, he was left feeling dead in the water, with no wind in his sails.

To be fair, some people don't process well out loud. They are internal processors and prefer to think options through before responding. But if the boss knew her report well, she would know he is a highly relational individual and that personal time and attention are invigorating for him. That she neither recognized his preferred style nor provided a rational explanation for her response left him frustrated. He felt he had no connection with her and was unimportant to her.

You don't have to be BFFs with your colleagues and reports to be an effective leader. In fact, you probably shouldn't be, unless such a relationship develops freely and authentically. But remember, while you are looking to those under you to get results, they are looking to you for a relationship. And time is a language of love.

Share Your Support

Nothing of long-lasting, positive value ever happens by force. Which is to say that command and control tactics, manipulation, threats, and leading through fear may work for a short season. But in the end, those types of approaches will be deemed ineffective as people revolt against such heavy-handed methods. These old-school methodologies are being phased out of most systems. And for good reason—they simply don't work for a sustainable period of time. Dwight Eisenhower is purported to have said that leading people by hitting them over the head is assault, not leadership.

Good leaders leverage influence rather than force. They are adept at connecting the passion of their people to the mission of the organization in such a way that it produces elevated performance. They leverage strengths. They grow to know what an individual is capable of contributing and then position that person for success in such a way that they can use their gifts and talents effectively. Good leaders don't mind moving people to different seats on the bus if it means increasing worker satisfaction.

> **Good leaders leverage influence rather than force. They are adept at connecting the passion of their people to the mission of the organization.**

Inspirational leaders also give free access to their knowledge, their network, and their resources in order to guarantee that those in their purview are well supported. They tee people up for success. They understand that the best way to become successful is to ensure the success of every team member. So, they don't let anyone flounder. Nor do they leave them on their own to find their way. They may not tell them directly how to get to a destination or specifically which route to take, but they provide them with a map, a compass, and companionship for the journey.

Good leaders provide opportunities for their team members to grow. They stretch them to venture out of their comfort zones. They do not delegate simply to get more work done. Instead, they use delegation as an instrument for growth and development. They assign tasks intentionally to allow team members to wrestle with new problems, forcing them to be resourceful and think creatively. They choose to appoint projects that will prepare their people for greater roles and responsibilities as their careers progress. And they offer the support and point them toward the resources that will ensure their success.

Share Your Relationships

One of the greatest resources you can provide for others is your network. Who do you know whom someone else needs to know? When you connect people who have commonality, you serve as a catalyst for creative activity. Most people are only a degree or two of separation away from success. And you may be just the person to connect the right people to one another for the benefit of one or both of them.

As we have discussed, NetWeaving is the art of connecting people who could benefit from knowing one another. Sometimes an introduction is an impactful gift. Move in your spheres of influence with the view to discover points of connection between people you know. Then share the relationship.

Share Your Knowledge

Another gift you can give is your knowledge. Your education, experiences, and relationships have provided you with a unique perspective and degree of mastery. Your legacy is created when you pass what you know along to others. One of the best means through which to do this is to mentor others. Teaching others not only imparts wisdom but also refines our thought processes as we share that knowledge. It benefits both the giver and the receiver.

People who have both a mentor and a mentee by and large demonstrate a desire to be engaged in continual learning. They also manifest more emotional health and greater happiness due to the depth of their relational connectivity. Find someone who is a little ahead of you in life, in their career, and in their maturity. Make sure they are someone you respect and would want to emulate. Remember, you become like the company you keep. So, your values align with theirs and you aren't seeking out someone solely for their success in business. Then ask if they would be so kind as to meet with you regularly for the purpose of imparting their wisdom.

> **Sometimes an introduction is an impactful gift.**

If they agree, then maximize every moment with that person. Everyone wants to feel as if their time is being wisely invested. Come to each meeting with an agenda and a short list of questions. Delve deeply into whatever subject matter you believe their wisdom would benefit you most. Mine the depths of their expertise to extract gems of insight. Always be respectful and grateful for their time.

Then turn around and do the same for someone else. Find someone in whom you may invest your time, insight, and energy. Look for others who are eager to learn, are teachable, and are willing to make themselves available. Invest in the growth of others.

For years now, I have met with a number of businessmen for this very purpose. A close friend and I have chosen to invite others into a learning experience in which we invest in one another. The two of us meet once a month for three hours with a group of approximately eight other men. The purpose of these meetings is relational, professional, and spiritual development. Each group meets for ten months. We have an agenda and everyone must read a specific book before attending each meeting. That serves as the primer for our discussions. We share insights, discuss challenges, provide encouragement, and sharpen one another. We are connected. We are growing. We are deeply known. We do life together, shoulder to shoulder and heart to heart.

Mentoring relationships allow you to do life together with others—deeply!

Share Your Story

Everyone has a story. And all our stories are interconnected. Our stories make us human. Your story is uniquely yours. It contains life experiences and lessons that others need to hear. Your successes can encourage others. Your challenges can inspire others. Your failures can provide helpful insight to help others avoid pitfalls. Your growth can guide others to find hope and resources to navigate their world more effectively.

Share your story freely. Not just the sanitized version—the authentic version. Be open and honest. And what you will find is that the more personal you think something to be, the more universal it actually is. In other words, everyone faces hardships, challenges, and pain. For many, that pain lies just beneath the surface. When we share our stories in an authentic fashion, we connect with others on a deeper level. We acknowledge our humanity. And we glean strength through being connected authentically with others. When we know others deeply and are known by others deeply, we become relationally rich and connected in genuine community. And that is vital.

Share Appreciation

Gratitude has a healing effect. Expressing appreciation on a regular basis combats envy and covetousness. It even serves as a deterrent to depression. Depression is often the result of disappointment, which can occur in the face of unmet expectations. When someone focuses on what they don't have to the exclusion of what they do have, they lose perspective. Gratitude causes a person to stop and contemplate the good things in life and reflect on how they became possible. It bursts the bubble of myopia and causes a person to consider how rich life is and how others have contributed to making their world a better place.

> **Expressing appreciation reinforces the fact that we do not operate in isolation but are interdependent.**

Expressing appreciation is a discipline that soothes the soul and brings joy to the heart. It reinforces the fact that we do not operate in isolation but are interdependent. Our success and happiness are tied to the success and happiness of others. Gratitude is characteristic of a disposition driven by humility. Pride says, "I did it!" Gratitude says, "Thanks, I couldn't have done it without you!"

Share the Love

Love is something you do. It's not just a warm sentiment. Love is action taken on behalf of another because you have their best interest at heart. It's not self-seeking. It's often sacrificial. It means doing what is right by another. Sometimes it involves affirmation. Sometimes it means confronting someone. Sometimes it involves giving. Sometimes it means setting limits and boundaries. But it always involves seeking the best for another.

Love does. Love does what is right. Love does what is best. Love does what creates the most value for everyone involved. Love does everything in the most personal and impactful way possible.

Love is patient. Love is kind. Love does not envy others but rather is grateful. It does not boast. It's not proud. Love does not dishonor others. It's not self-seeking. It's not easily angered. Love keeps no record of wrongs, because love forgives. Love does not deal in falsehood but stands on the side of truth. Love protects. Love trusts. Love hopes. Love perseveres. Love conquers all.

May the Influence Be with You

In the *Star Wars* movies, the Force holds the universe together. Both good and evil constitute the Force. Individuals must either choose to align themselves with the light side or be taken over by the dark side of the Force. Power, domination, and manipulation are the weapons of the dark side, all seeking the destruction of any resistance coming from the side of light. For the dark side, force replaces influence. Hatred quells compassion. Self-promotion and self-interest are the path to greatness, using both people and resources for one's personal benefit. Forced compliance holds the dark side together.

But leadership based on force is not sustainable. Nothing of long-lasting, positive value ever happens by force. Eventually, people will resist conformity. A sense of personal responsibility, accountability, and passion provide cohesion for the side of light. Those who share their time, support, relationships, knowledge, stories, appreciation, and love will enlighten the workforce.

Leadership is influence. It's inspiring people to create value for others in each and every encounter. It's not about self-interest, self-promotion, or self-service.

Good leadership leaves a positive wake in the world. The best leaders serve. And, those leaders who serve make other people's stories better. They leave an indelible impression on others that cannot easily be erased. They are by all accounts remarkable!

> **Nothing of long-lasting, positive value ever happens by force.**

May *the Influence be with you* to serve others well and bring light to the world.

>> **GAINING TRACTION: Questions for Consideration & Application**

1. What are some practical ways you can better share your time with your team members?

2. What introductions could you make for your team members that might expose them to helpful people and resources?

3. How can you more effectively share your knowledge with team members?

4. What part of your story might you share with your team members to inspire, encourage, or challenge them?

5. What are a few fresh ways you might be able to share your appreciation with your team members?

6. How can you better love your team members?

SIXTEEN

POWERED BY
RELATIONSHIPS

We must learn to live together as brothers or perish together
as fools.

—Martin Luther King Jr.

F or years, researchers have been attempting to defini-
tively determine what factors lead to a happy and
productive life. For over seventy-five years, Harvard's
Grant and Glueck studies have tracked the psychosocial
predictors of healthy aging among two populations. The
Grant Study is composed of 268 Harvard graduates from
the classes of 1939 to 1944. The Glueck Study group is made
up of 456 men who grew up in the inner-city neighborhoods

of Boston. These studies have been particularly focused on what psychosocial variables and biological processes from earlier in life predict health and well-being among those who live into their eighties and nineties. This longitudinal study is now beginning to examine the children of the original participants.[1]

Since before World War II, researchers have diligently analyzed blood samples, conducted brain scans, pored over self-reported surveys, and dissected interpersonal interactions with these men to compile their findings. Their conclusion is resounding and singular. According to Robert Waldinger, director of the Harvard Study of Adult Development, "The clearest message that we get from this seventy-five-year study is this: good relationships keep us happier and healthier. Period."[2]

Happiness has little to do with how much money we have in our savings account. Happiness has nothing to do with the level of our education or how many titles we have attained professionally. The biggest predictor of happiness and fulfillment overall is how we experience love in relationship. Specifically, the study demonstrates that having healthy, close relationships helps our nervous system relax and our brain stay active longer as well as reduces emotional and physical pain. The data also shows very clearly that those who feel lonely or isolated are more likely to see their physical health decline earlier and die younger.

> **Happiness has nothing to do with the level of our education or how many titles we have attained professionally.**

According to Waldinger, "It's not just the number of friends you have, and it's not whether or not you're in a committed relationship. It's the quality of your close relationships that matters."[3] Are your relationships marked by vulnerability and enduring depth? Do you feel safe sharing your real self rather than pretending to be someone you are not? Can you relax and enjoy being with others despite your imperfections and theirs? Are both people committed to extending grace and working through conflict without attacking each other's character? Is there accountability and forgiveness? These are the marks of mature relationships.

George Vaillant is the Harvard psychiatrist who directed the study from 1972 to 2004. According to Vaillant, these healthy relationships have two foundational elements. "One is love. The other is finding a way of coping with life that does not push love away," says Vaillant.[4]

Love is not a soft and fuzzy word. Love, as we have seen, is acting in someone else's best interest. When we love others deeply and allow them to love us deeply, life is transformed. This is true personally and corporately. The best leaders know how to love well. They are purpose-driven, valuecentric, and deeply compassionate.

Good leaders know that corporate success is determined by how well we play in the sandbox together. Healthy relationships internally will drive healthy relationships with customers. Healthy relationships make an organization remarkable. *Remarkable* describes those who are others-focused. They go above and beyond in providing stellar service. They are intent on making someone's story a little better. They exceed all expectations. They love well. They create value at a world-class level. And they do so to such a degree that those they encounter have an irrepressible desire to tell others about their experience. And when others leave their presence talking about how they have positively impacted lives, then indeed they have become remarkable.

Corporate culture is an expression of the health of relationships. Leaders must be wholeheartedly committed to providing the resources necessary to cultivate strong and lasting relationships among individuals and teams if they want their efforts to be sustainable. Ultimately, clarity and unity are the result of healthy relationships. Clarity and unity will lead to productivity. Likewise, the quality of relationships will determine customer loyalty.

Relational integrity produces cohesiveness and collaboration. Depth and transparency of relationship contributes to retaining top-talent in the life of the organization. When healthy relationships are present, people find fulfillment in their work and productivity soars. When relationships are rich, people are simply happier. Business, to be effective, must be powered by healthy relationships.

In the end, you can have all the money you've ever desired, a successful career, and good physical health. But without loving, healthy relationships, life will feel incomplete. The next time you find yourself scrolling through Facebook instead of being present at the table, stop and engage with those around you. If you're considering staying late once again at the office instead of being home for dinner with the family or getting together with friends, then stop and reconsider. If you begin to treat people as assets to the organization rather than valued individuals who are worthy of your time and attention, then reassess your leadership. If you find yourself hiring with little commitment to the long-term growth and development of team members, then revamp the system. If you begin to feel as though leadership is a solo endeavor, then slow down and spend more time cultivating connectedness with others.

Dedicate yourself to creating a culture in which there is a strong commitment to relational integrity. Become a value creator, intent on not only bringing your best to every endeavor but also insisting that everyone else do the same. Intercept entropy early and engage in RAW developmental conversations. Become a ninja of conflict resolution. Lead beyond self and love deeply. Create a safe environment in which people can be themselves and find the resources they need to accelerate personal growth and professional development.

> **If you begin to feel as though leadership is a solo endeavor, then slow down and spend more time cultivating connectedness with others.**

Relationships can be complicated. But, in the end, relationship catalyzes growth. The good life is built on good relationships. Personal happiness and fulfillment are found in maturing relationships. And thriving businesses are powered by relationships.

>> **GAINING TRACTION: Questions for Consideration & Application**

1. What are the most impactful principles you have gleaned from this book?

2. Which principles have you already been able to apply and what impact have they had?

3. Where would you most like to grow as a leader? What steps do you plan to take to enhance your leadership capabilities?

4. How has your thinking shifted as a result of reading *Relationomics*?

5. Who do you know who could benefit from being exposed to this content?

GLOSSARY OF TERMS

Culture—The collective expression of the values, beliefs, and behaviors individuals bring to any endeavor. It's the manifestation of communal priorities and how people choose to relate to one another. Simply stated, it is how we play in the sandbox with one another.

Emotional intelligence—The degree to which someone has the ability to both read and lead oneself and others. Self-awareness and authenticity are cornerstones of emotional intelligence. A high degree of emotional intelligence carries with it the capacity to know, own, and be responsible for one's feelings, thoughts, and actions.

Grounded leader—Someone who is emotionally mature and stable, firmly rooted in convictions and steadfast in determination. Grounded leaders demonstrate the following characteristics: rooted in reality, emotionally centered, relationally rich, results-oriented, others-focused, mission-minded.

Growth Spiral—A means whereby an individual may assess whether they are engaging for growth or resisting change. One may either ascend the spiral toward growth and transformation or descend the spiral toward desperation and alienation. Each takes place in a progression of spirals.

Growth gear—The state of being relationally engaged for growth by embracing feedback and acting responsibly. It's a disposition of seeking to create the most value for everyone involved.

Luciferianism—A belief system that reveres enlightenment, independence, and human progression. Sometimes mistakenly associated with Satanism due to the Christian interpretation of the fallen angel. This philosophical approach stresses enlightenment as the ultimate goal and highlights freedom of will, worshiping the inner self, and the fulfillment of one's personal potential.

NetWeaving—A term, coined by Bob Littell, that stands in contrast to networking. Creating value by connecting others who share a common interest or may be able to serve one another in a mutually beneficial manner. NetWeaving is gratuitously providing information or resources as a way of building relationships. It is about promoting someone else's story above one's own. It is an understanding that all the good things we desire in life are by-products of creating value for others.

OAR—The elements that must be present for team members to bring their best to the table in each endeavor. OAR is an acrostic, which stands for: ownership, accountability, and responsibility.

Pipeline vs. platform—Traditional learning systems are essentially *pipelines*. There is a reservoir of content, which is pushed from a repository to a recipient. It's a one-way flow of information that the sender hopes the recipient will ingest, thus providing the diet of information for growth to take place. But, devoid of relationship, it rarely garners the intended result.

A *platform*, on the other hand, provides a stage for interaction for those who have been enlisted in a learning community. Information flows freely back and forth, allowing all participants to move fluidly between the modalities of learning, applying, and teaching. This learning triangle produces an environment of friendship and reinforcement. Because information is shared in the context of community and encouragement, learning takes place at a rapid pace and application is celebrated among members of the learning community.

RAW conversation—A productive developmental conversation. RAW is an acrostic, which incorporates the three components of this type of coaching conversation: reality, advancement, and wrestling.

Relationomics—The study of the observable impact that relationships have on economic activity. It's an assessment of the value created by relationships as opposed to simply a fiscal transactional analysis. In the marketplace, there is a significant causal correlation between the strength of the relationship and the flow of resources. The stronger and healthier the relationship, the more productive and profitable the transactions between those parties tend to be.

Remarkable culture—An environment in which people:
Believe the best *in* one another,
Want the best *for* one another, and
Expect the best *from* one another.

Self-Help Conundrum—The fanciful idea that one may attain maturity apart from being relationally connected with others. We are all interconnected. By nature, we are relational creatures and relationships help hone us to maturity. Maturity is marked by how well we relate to others. Growth does not take place in a relational vacuum.

Self-Transcendence—Living beyond self. It's focusing on what you can do for others. It's creating a legacy of good. It's seeking to meet the needs of others and, in doing so, finding meaning and fulfillment in life personally. It's also counterintuitive; the secret to leading a meaningful and fulfilling life is actually found in generosity. The more you give, the more you will receive.

Valucentricity—The energy and momentum that is produced when values are properly identified and aligned, producing a unified and energized workforce.

NOTES

Chapter 1 This Is a Relationship!

1. David Maraniss, *When Pride Still Mattered: A Life of Vince Lombardi* (New York: Touchstone, 2000), 274–76.

Chapter 2 The Great Deception

1. See Genesis 3.

2. James P. Comer (lecture, Education Service Center, Houston, TX, 1995).

3. James P. Comer, *Leave No Child Behind: Preparing Today's Youth for Tomorrow's World* (New Haven, CT: Yale University Press, 2005), 1–62.

Chapter 3 Myopia Is No Utopia

1. Stephen C. Byrum, *From the Neck Up: The Recovery and Sustaining of the Human Element in Modern Organizations* (Littleton, MA: Tapestry Press, 2004), 9–27.

Chapter 4 The Culture Conversation

1. Edwin Friedman, *A Failure of Nerve: Leadership in the Age of the Quick Fix* (New York: Church Publishing, 2017), 196.

Chapter 5 Nobody Is Normal

1. *Young Frankenstein*, directed by Mel Brooks (Los Angeles, CA: Twentieth Century Fox, 1974).

2. Dictionary.com, s.v. "normal," accessed July 30, 2018, https://www.dictionary.com/browse/normal?s=t.

3. Dictionary.com, s.v. "asset," accessed July 30, 2018, https://www.dict ionary.com/browse/normal?s=t.

Chapter 6 The Growth Spiral

1. Antonio Damasio, *Descartes' Error* (New York: Putnam Berkley Group, 1994), 52–58.

Chapter 7 Face Value

1. Travis Bradberry, *Emotional Intelligence 2.0* (San Diego: TalentSmart, 2009), 13–23.

2. Robert S. Littell, *The Heart and Art of NetWeaving: Building Meaningful Relationships One Connection at a Time* (Atlanta: NetWeaving International Press, 2006), 12–20.

3. *Jerry Maguire*, directed by Cameron Crowe (Los Angeles, CA: Gracie Films, 1996).

Chapter 8 Fear Factor

1. "Ignacy Jan Paderewski," Youth.dadabhagwan.org, accessed July 30, 2018, http://youth.dadabhagwan.org/youth-in-action/glimpses-of-great-souls /ignacy-jan-paderewski-1/.

2. "Herbert Hoover and Poland," Independence Hall Association, July 4, 1995, http://www.ushistory.org/more/hoover.htm.

3. Abraham Maslow, *Motivation and Personality*, ed. Robert Frager, James Fadiman, Cynthia McReynolds, and Ruth Cox (Vision Book Distributors, 1987), 23–48.

4. Mark E. Kolto-Rivera, "Discovering the Later Version of Maslow's Hierarchy of Needs: Self-Transcendence and Opportunities for Theory, Research, and Unification," *Review of General Psychology* 10, no. 4 (2006): 302–17.

5. George Bernard Shaw, *Candida* (Auckland: The Floating Press, 2010), 13.

6. Laura Geggel, "Super Schnozzle: Thin, Glow-in-the-Dark Shark Has a Huge Nose," LiveScience, July 31, 2017, https://www.livescience.com/59 983-tiny-shark-glows.html.

Chapter 9 Row, Row, Row Your Boat

1. Peter F. Drucker, "What Makes an Effective Executive," *Harvard Business Review*, June 2004, https://hbr.org/2004/06/what-makes-an-effective -executive.

Chapter 10 Rules of Engagement

1. Michael Walzer, *Just and Unjust Wars* (New York: Basic Books, 2015), 38–39.

Chapter 11 RAW Conversations

1. Randall Beck and Jim Harter, "Why Great Managers Are So Rare," *Business Journal*, March 25, 2014, http://news.gallup.com/businessjournal/167975/why-great-managers-rare.aspx.

Chapter 12 Re:Solution

1. Eleanor Roosevelt, "My Day—August 2, 1941," My Day Project, George Washington University, accessed June 18, 2018, https://www2.gwu.edu/~erpapers/myday/displaydoc.cfm?_y=1941&_f=md055954.

2. C. Stephen Byrum, *From the Neck Up: The Recovery and Sustaining of the Human Element in Modern Organizations* (Littleton, MA: Tapestry Press, Ltd, 2006), 47–50.

3. José Emilio Pacheco, *Battles in the Desert and Other Stories* (New York: New Directions, 1987).

4. Viktor E. Frankl, *Man's Search for Meaning* (Boston: Beacon Press, 2006), 140.

5. Frankl, *Man's Search*, 65–72.

6. Frankl, 110–11.

7. Frankl, 165.

Chapter 13 Leadership beyond Self-Interest

1. "The Chobani Way: Committed to the Planet and Its People," Chobani, accessed June 19, 2018, https://www.chobani.com/impact/the-chobani-way.

2. Megan Durisin, "Chobani CEO: Our Success Has Nothing to Do with Yogurt," PRI, May 3, 2013, https://www.pri.org/stories/2013-05-03/chobani-ceo-our-success-has-nothing-do-yogurt.

3. Stephanie Strom, "At Chobani, Now It's Not Just the Yogurt That's Rich," *New York Times*, April 27, 2016, https://www.nytimes.com/2016/04/27/business/a-windfall-for-chobani-employees-stakes-in-the-company.html.

4. Mark A. Weinberger, "Hamdi Ulukaya, Founder and CEO, Chobani, Inc. and EY World Entrepreneur Of The Year™ 2013 Award winner, interviewed by Mark A. Weinberger, EY Global Chairman & CEO," Ernst & Young, November 16, 2013, https://www.ey.com/us/en/services/strategic-growth-markets/strategic-growth-forum-agenda-2013-evtd-usdd-98smd9.

5. Ergulen Toprak, "Chobani's Founder Gives $300 Million to Employees," MyReports, May 2, 2016, https://myreportsny.com/2016/05/02/chobanis-founder-gives-300-millions-to-employees/.

6. Victoria Craig, "Chobani Founder: The American Dream Happened to Me," FOX Business, February 18, 2014, https://www.foxbusiness.com/features/chobani-founder-the-american-dream-happened-to-me.

7. Nina Roberts, "Chobani's Founder Hamdi Ulukaya Reveals the Simple Secret to Strong Branding," *Forbes*, September 29, 2017, https://www.forbes.com/sites/ninaroberts/2017/09/29/chobanis-founder-hamdi-ulukaya-reveals-the-simple-secret-to-strong-branding-just-be-real/#323489d5b174.

Chapter 14 Closing the Revolving Door

1. Robert S. Hartman, *The Structure of Value* (Eugene, OR: Wipf and Stock, 2011), 19–36.

2. Sean McCracken, "From Ritz to Capella, Schulze Redefines Luxury," Hotel News Now, December 4, 2015, http://www.hotelnewsnow.com/Articles/28703/From-Ritz-to-Capella-Schulze-redefines-luxury.

3. Doug Gollan, "The Second Act of Horst Schulze Is Finally Taking Off," *Forbes*, June 1, 2016, https://www.forbes.com/sites/douggollan/2016/06/01/the-second-act-of-horst-schulze-is-finally-taking-off/3/#54269dce4496.

4. Gollan, "The Second Act of Horst Schulze Is Finally Taking Off."

Chapter 15 Leading with Love

1. *Star Wars: The Last Jedi*, directed by Rian Johnson (San Francisco, CA: Lucasfilm, 2017).

Chapter 16 Powered by Relationships

1. "Study of Adult Development," Harvard Second Generation Study, accessed June 21, 2018, http://www.adultdevelopmentstudy.org/grantandglueckstudy.

2. Marguerite Ward, "75-Year Harvard Study Reveals the Key to Success in 2017 and Beyond," CNBC, December 15, 2016, https://www.cnbc.com/2016/12/15/75-year-harvard-study-reveals-the-key-to-success-in-2017-and-beyond.html.

3. Ward, "75-Year Harvard Study."

4. George E. Vaillant and Kenneth Mukamal, "Successful Aging," *American Journal of Psychiatry* 158, no. 6 (June 2001): 839–47.

ACKNOWLEDGMENTS

I am a rich man. Not because my bank statement attests to that fact. Frankly, my tax return is fairly simple. But I am rich because of the multitude of people who have invested their time, knowledge, and energy in my growth process. I have been greatly influenced by some remarkable people, and, consequently, I am relationally rich. It would not be possible to list them all at this time. But there are a few who have contributed significantly to this project and an expression of gratitude is in order. So, please allow me to thank:

My wife, LuAnne, and family. Thanks for your belief in me—and this project—along with your patience and understanding for all the hours I barricaded myself in "the loft." Much of what I know about relationships, I have learned because of you.

My agent, Chris Ferebee. I want to express my gratitude for your friendship, encouragement, and support. It makes it easier having you in my corner.

Jennifer Leep, Chad Allen, Eileen Hanson, Amy Ballor, and the entire Baker team for your guidance and grace through the entire process of refining and positioning this book to reach a broader audience. I am grateful for your expertise.

My editor, Michelle Rapkin. Once again it was an honor and a privilege to work together with you on crafting this content so that it was fluid and impactful. I am grateful for your uncanny ability to take my complex, rambling thoughts and synthesize them to help me state them clearly. I so appreciate your grasp of grammar and the English language.

David Salyers, my coauthor for *Remarkable!* Thanks for helping me flesh out the concept of *Relationomics* and for allowing me to use the term as the title.

Randy Walton, my business partner at Remarkable! I am grateful for your strategic mind. Thank you for allowing me the privilege of partnering with you as we impart these principles to our client base.

Duane Cummings for your advice, example, and ongoing encouragement. Your capacity to connect people in meaningful relationships continues to inspire me.

Scott MacLellan, Robby Angle, Bob Kilinski, Dave Hare, Jim Leath, Kevin Latty, Ron Dunn, Charles Buffington, and Bob Littell for your feedback that helped shape and sharpen this content. And for each of you being cheerleaders of the message. I am blessed to have you in my life.

Our friends and clients, who continually make the case for the efficacy of these principles as they apply them to enrich relationships and drive business. It's truly a pleasure to learn with you. Thank you for entrusting us with the privilege of investing in your teams.

Dr. Randy Ross is founder and CEO (Chief Enthusiasm Officer) of Remarkable!, a corporate advisory and consulting firm specializing in talent selection, cultural development, and organizational health. Randy is a craftsman of culture and a catalytic coach who inspires elevated performance. A master of cultural transformation, he has a unique understanding of employee engagement and offers practical solutions for increasing both the morale and productivity of teams.

Spending time in both the for-profit and not-for-profit worlds, Randy has traveled throughout the United States and internationally as a speaker, consultant, and coach, building teams and developing leaders. A compelling communicator, he has the keen sensitivity to speak into the hearts of leaders.

He and his wife, LuAnne, live in Johns Creek, Georgia, and have four children (Ryan, Lindsay, Colton, and Jonathan). They enjoy traveling, sailing, and participating in a wide array of athletic activities.

Connect with
DR. RANDY ROSS

For additional resources, visit **www.CreateRemarkable.com** and **www.RemarkableMovement.com**.

For speaking engagements, visit **www.DrRandyRoss.com**.

ROADMAP TO REMARKABLE

Digital Edition

The Roadmap to Remarkable Digital Edition is designed to allow leaders to take their teams on a developmental journey while connected on an enhanced smartphone platform. Applying the content from *REMARKABLE!*, the app allows participants to grow in community by utilizing a wide array of interactive resources. It also allows leaders to engage with their teams in ongoing developmental conversation.

"A platform rich with community, content, and engagement tools that help your influence continue beyond the face-to-face."

"The R! app brings together content and community to power growth and give you the tools to create a Remarkable! culture."

Act Now to Begin Your Remarkable! Journey

To learn more and sign up for a Mini-Journey of Remarkable! simply access the app store for your mobile device and:

- Download the Remarkable app
- Create an account
- Enter the invite code: "BeRemarkable"